social media IN SPORT MARKETING

Timothy Newman *YORK COLLEGE OF PENNSYLVANIA*

Jason Frederick Peck *LIVINGSOCIAL*

Charles Harris *CALIFORNIA STATE UNIVERSITY, LONG BEACH*

Brendan Wilhide *@BRENDANWILHIDE*

Consulting Editor: Packianathan Chelladurai

...blishers
...e, Arizona
H·H·P

Library of Congress Cataloging-in-Publication Data

Newman, Timothy.
  Social media in sport marketing / Timothy Newman, Jason Frederick Peck,
Charles Harris, Brendan Wilhide.
    p. cm.
  Includes bibliographical references and index.
  ISBN 978-1-934432-93-8 (ebook) — ISBN 978-1-934432-78-5 (print book)   1.
Sports—Marketing.   2. Sports—Computer network resources.   3. Social
media.
I. Title.
  GV716.N48 2013
  338.47796—dc23

                                                              2013004173

Please note: The authors and publisher have made every effort to provide current
website addresses in this book. However, because web addresses change constantly,
it is inevitable that some of the URLs listed here will change following publication.

Holcomb Hathaway, Publishers, Inc.
8700 E. Via de Ventura Blvd., Suite 265
Scottsdale, Arizona 85258
480-991-7881
www.hh-pub.com

10 9 8 7 6 5 4 3 2 1

Print ISBN: 978-1-934432-78-5

contents

CHAPTER 4

Blogging   69

CHAPTER 7

Mobile Marketing   135

CHAPTER 8

Email Marketing   157

CHAPTER 9

Planning and Measuring a Successful Social Media Program   173

Not surprisingly, companies of all sizes are using social media as part of their marketing and public relations efforts. The growth of the social media phenomenon and constant advances in technology obviously create unique and powerful opportunities for those able to capitalize on them. The question is how best to do so? *Social Media in Sport Marketing* has been created to help answer this question as it pertains to sport organizations. Our goal is to create one compact resource to address the needs of students learning about social media platforms and tools specifically for sport marketing and sport communication. It is written from the perspective of the sport professional, and the examples, case studies, and applications originate specifically from the world of sports.

Social Media in Sport Marketing explores sport marketing goals in relation to social media tools and concepts being used today. While the specific media platforms used may change over time, the marketing goals behind their use, and many of the foundational tools such as real time blogging, images, and videos, are here to stay. This book gives readers a thorough understanding of the key components of social media, teaches individuals how to use social media to develop professional as well as personal brands, and discusses the role of social media to increase an organization's reach and revenue.

Chapters 1 and 2 offer background regarding the rise of social media and the principles of sport communication and marketing as they relate to social media. Chapter 3 discusses social networks and real-time platforms. Chapters 4 and 5 cover blogging, livestreaming, podcasting, and related tools such as images and videos. Chapters 6 through 8 focus on mobile marketing, search marketing, and email marketing, all of which are all crucial to an organization's success in today's digital world. Throughout, the text covers the key challenges and issues sport marketers face while implementing social media campaigns. Finally, the text concludes with a chapter on planning a social media program and the crucial step of measuring the effectiveness of social media efforts.

To reinforce key concepts, chapters contain specific examples, web resources, and case studies drawn from sport organizations and social media front-runners. The authors' collective personal and professional experiences allow readers to learn from the successes and failures of practitioners dealing with social media and sports in the real world. On this book's website, www.hhpcommunities.com/sportmanagement, the sport-related case studies and review questions will be supplemented with online materials offering updates, specific examples, and timely illustrations that reinforce the book's content.

When a social media program is planned properly, integrated into an organization's business objectives, and aligned with other marketing efforts, an organization can expect increased customer loyalty and revenue. The goal of this book is to help readers use social media effectively to market to customers and build relationships that will ideally benefit both parties.

ACKNOWLEDGMENTS

We started the process of writing this book in order to address the need for a resource for both practitioners and students. The journey has taught us more than we expected, and we have all benefited along the way. As a result, we would like to thank Holcomb Hathaway for believing in and supporting this project. Special thanks go to Lauren Salas, who got us started, encouraged our work, and guided us through the beginning stages of the project. Colette Kelly provided us with continual support and guidance, while Gay Pauley helped tremendously in the final stages of editing and producing the chapters.

We want to thank the book's reviewers, who offered constructive suggestions for improving it. Thanks to Khalid Ballouli, University of South Carolina; Wayne Blann, Ithaca College; Cheri Bradish, Brock University; Kevin Byon, University of Georgia; Andrew Choi, University of San Francisco; Beth Cianfrone, Georgia State University; Ronald Dick, Duquesne University; Brendan Dwyer, Virginia Commonwealth University; Kevin Filo, University of Massachusetts; Meredith Geisler, American University; Gregory Greenhalgh, Virginia Commonwealth University; Chris Greenwell, University of Louisville; Cody T. Havard, University of Memphis; Mike Hyman, New Mexico State University; Patricia Kennedy, University of Nebraska-Lincoln; Nicholas Lorgnier, Canisius College; Joseph E. Mahan, Temple University; Robert Malekoff,

Guilford College; Kimberly Miloch, Texas Woman's University; Linda Schoenstedt, College of Mount St. Joseph; and Kyle Woody, Ithaca College. The book is better as a result of their efforts.

I would personally like to thank Hank Steinbrecher for his willingness to share his stories and ideas; Joe Favorito for his time, encouragement and guidance; and my colleagues for encouraging me to pursue this project. A special thank you goes to Pat Massa, who has been the best mentor anyone could ask for both personally and professionally. I must also thank all of my students, past and present, for challenging me to be the best as I challenge them day after day.

   Thank you to my family and friends for their suggestions and guidance, especially Mike Steinagel for always getting me back on track by giving me a different perspective and putting a smile on my face. Thank you to my in-laws and brother-in-law for their understanding and support. Thank you to my mom and dad, who have always supported and believed in me, no matter what. Thanks to my brothers for all of their love and the many competitions we had growing up, which fostered my perseverance and drive. To Katie and Beth, the best daughters I could ever ask for, remember the world is yours for the taking—work hard and your dreams will come true. To my wife, Jen, thank you for your love, patience, and help with this book. Without your support, none of this is possible. —*TN*

Thank you to my wife, Sneha, for all of her support and encouragement. Thank you to my parents for inspiring me and helping me develop a willingness to work hard and pursue interesting things. —*JP*

I want to thank my family, Isabelle, Tal, and Yael, and my father and sister, for all of their love, support, and understanding. I would also like to thank the California State University, Long Beach, Sport Management Program for their support and guidance during this project. —*CH*

I would like to thank my mom and dad (Kate and Tim) and the rest of the family for always believing in me. I would also like to thank Sara for her patience during the writing and editing stages and for her encouragement throughout the process. —*BW*

Tim Newman is currently an associate professor at York College of Pennsylvania. Tim earned his doctorate in sport management at the United States Sports Academy, his master's degree in education at the University of Virginia, and his bachelor's degree from Towson University. He also serves as a member of the United States Sports Academy's national faculty, working with distance learning students and teaching courses in Botswana, Malaysia, and Thailand. Tim actively contributes his time to a variety of professional organizations, community projects, and volunteer programs each year and recently accepted positions on the National Board of Directors for the Leaders of Tomorrow Foundation and the Board of Commissioners for the Commission on Sport Management Accreditation. As an avid golfer, Tim participates in competitive golf each year and is a director of the Golfweek Amateur Tour in the Washington, D.C., metro area. Tim's primary areas of research include marketing, social media, social networking, and issues related to leadership. His interests and areas of expertise culminated in the creation of the Dream Chasers Management Group, which he founded in 2011. Tim currently lives in Pennsylvania with his wife and enjoys spending time with his two children.

Jason Peck is a social media strategist with business-to-business and business-to-consumer experience in sports, entertainment, and ecommerce. Jason works at LivingSocial, where he focuses on social media and online marketing for the company's one-of-a-kind experiences and events. He also serves as Vice President of Digital Content and Community for the Washington, DC, chapter of the Social Media Club, the world's largest community of social media professionals. He graduated from the University of North Carolina at Chapel Hill and is a die-hard Tar Heel basketball fan. Jason currently lives in Arlington, Virginia, and occasionally writes at www.jasonfpeck.com.

Charles Harris has enjoyed a successful sport management career, having worked in college athletics, professional baseball, and professional hockey. Charles previously served on senior management teams with the Los Angeles Dodgers, the Anaheim Ducks, and the University of California, Irvine, Anteaters, and as an assistant with the Anaheim Angels. He also has extensive experience in the technology sector, first serving as president and founder of an Israel-based marketing and communications firm and later as a marketing technology consultant to top U. S. companies. During his time abroad, Charles owned the rights to market Major League Baseball in several Middle Eastern countries and territories. A graduate of the University of California, Irvine, Charles has also served as an adjunct professor in the sport management graduate program at California State University, Long Beach, since 2004.

Brendan Wilhide is an emarketing and copywriting specialist at ForeSite Technologies in Connecticut and a contributing writer for *Macworld* and Macworld.com. He served as play-by-play broadcaster and public relations coordinator for a number of minor league baseball teams including Ripken Baseball's Aberdeen Iron-Birds and the Vermont Expos. His work cataloging the sports industry as part of his Sportsin140.com website project was featured in the *Wall Street Journal* and on ESPN's "Outside the Lines." He is a graduate of York College of Pennsylvania with a degree in Professional Writing. Follow him on Twitter: @BrendanWilhide

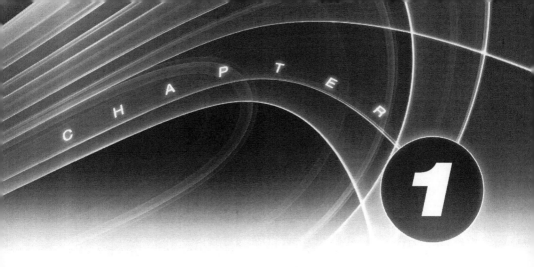

Introduction to Social Media

INTRODUCTION

Welcome to the world of social media. Changing media and technology have transformed the way we communicate with friends and family and how we consume information. Social media has also greatly affected the way organizations communicate and market to their audiences. As sport managers, it's important that we understand how social media is affecting the sport industry and what opportunities exist to reach fans.

In this chapter, we'll introduce you to some basic definitions and concepts of social media. We'll also cover the main types of social media platforms and technologies, to give you an idea of what to expect when we cover a few of them in more depth later in the book. We'll explore the history and rise of social media and examine its impact on individuals and organizations. While we believe the good far outweighs the bad, we would be remiss not to take a look at a few potential negative consequences of social media.

The goal of this book is to provide the background and guidance necessary to apply the best practices in the areas of the principles of marketing, communications, and social media to the field of sport. As you read this book, probably the best method for learning about social media is to *participate* in the process by experiencing social networking as both a *producer* and a *consumer.*

We start this chapter by giving you a basic understanding of social media from a marketing perspective and have you start coming up with your own ideas about it. You most likely interact with social media in your daily life, but you may not have thought about how it functions as a marketing or public relations tool or how it relates to the sport industry. This overview ensures we are all on the same social media page and prepares you for the more in-depth material in the following chapters.

WHAT IS SOCIAL MEDIA?

According to Safko and Brake (2009), the term *social media* encompasses all of the interactions between people online—all the ways they participate in and share information, knowledge, and opinions while using web-based applications to communicate. David Griner (2009), director of digital content with Luckie & Company, defines social media as "digital tools that let you share information and network with others" (unpaged).

In today's society, the 24-hour news cycle, technological innovations, and the pervasiveness of instant communication (cell phones, texting, and wi-fi) have altered the traditional concept of media. The umbrella term *media* has generally referred to the group of organizations and their employees who are regarded as the legitimate couriers of information. "Mainstream" media typically includes television, radio, newspapers, magazines, communication conglomerates, government agencies, and even research institutions as well as television personalities, radio broadcasters, reporters, journalists, and so forth.

Long gone, however, are the days when the public had only the mainstream media to provide them with news and content. With today's technology, information now moves in both directions between content providers and audiences. Using social media, people outside the mainstream media can easily create, edit, and post information online. As Joseph Thornley, CEO of Thornley Fallis, stated, "individuals shift fluidly and flexibly between the role of audience and author" (Thornley, 2008). In effect, anyone can become a "citizen journalist" or "marketing maven" by disseminating information via the Internet (Safko & Brake, 2009, p. 4). As a result, Griner asserts the rise of social media has in effect ended centuries of separation between mass media and the masses and removed barriers that separated businesses from their potential customers.

Social media enables us to watch and share videos and photos, read and write blogs, post on social networking sites, and have online conversations. As you can surmise from these activities, social media is a broad term for the various tools, platforms, and content that enable people to create, exchange, and consume information. Essentially, social media enables consumers to communicate in more efficient and effective ways than we were able to in the past. We asked a few professionals to describe social media in 140 characters or less. Exhibit 1.1 includes a few of their responses.

SOCIAL MEDIA WEBSITES, TOOLS, AND PLATFORMS

S ocial media is powered by a variety of platforms, tools, and technologies. These platforms and websites may have a single function, such as providing the means for people and organizations to share a specific type of content (e.g., videos). Or, they may have multiple purposes, such as bringing people together so they can share ideas and thoughts in a variety of content formats.

While there is definitely overlap among various types of social media, we identify three main categories of social media:

1. Publishing services
2. Media sharing services
3. Networking services

EXHIBIT 1.1   Social media in 140 characters: What the experts say.

"Social media is a tool that allows connection between humans with a reach never available before."

Stacey Alexander, Social Media Strategist at Media Two Interactive

"A digital form of communication that has the potential to be shared with others."

Jackie Adkins, Account Coordinator at GMR Marketing

"Social media is communication. Takes the many to the 1 to one dynamic and makes it a 2-way convo bt ppl, companies, orgs."

Chelsea Marti, Social Media Director at Automatic Data Processing

Here are brief definitions of each of these categories and examples of platforms that fall under each of them.

Publishing Services

Publishing services make it easy for people to publish information and ideas online. Examples of social media publishing services include blogs, forums, and wikis.

Blogs

Blogs are regularly updated websites (or sections of websites) where the content is presented in reverse-chronological order, with the newest stories at the top. Blogs usually allow people to leave comments on stories they've read. The tone and writing style of the blog may be formal or informal. There are no real rules; it's up to the blog owner or author to decide what to publish. *Example:* www.washingtonwizardsblog.com, the official blog of the Washington Wizards.

Forums

Forums, or message boards, are similar to blogs, but they differ in one major way. While blogs are usually only updated by one or a few authors, forums allow anyone who is a member to post content. *Example:* http://mbd.scout.com/mb.aspx?s=78&f=1408, a forum for University of North Carolina basketball fans.

Wikis

Wikis are websites built on a platform that enables individuals to easily create and edit multiple pages and link them together. Instead of a typical website, where the viewer has no ability to edit stories, wikis typically give readers the ability to edit stories and add to them. *Example:* http://armchairgm.wikia.com/Main_Page, the Armchair GM Wiki for all aspects of sports.

Media Sharing Services

Media sharing services enable people and organizations to share original content in a variety of formats online. They have also made it easier for people to save and share links to others' content. Examples of media sharing services include the following.

Social news websites

Social news websites enable people to submit links to news stories and vote on which ones they enjoy the most. Usually, the front pages of these sites will include the most popular news stories, as voted on by people. *Example:* http://www.reddit.com/r/sports.

Social bookmarking sites

Social bookmarking websites enable people to save and review links to stories, pictures, videos, and other content they find interesting. People can usually use tags, or descriptive keywords and phrases, to categorize various types of links. The social component of these sites is that people often can see what links their friends are tagging and bookmarking. *Example:* www.stumbleupon.com.

Video-sharing sites

Video-sharing sites are focused primarily on letting people upload and share videos they've created. Many of these sites also let people share their opinions on videos they watch by rating, starring, liking, or commenting on them. *Example:* www.youtube.com.

Photo-sharing sites

Photo-sharing sites allow people to post and organize pictures they've taken and leave feedback on others' pictures. *Example:* www.flickr.com.

Audio-sharing sites

Audio-sharing sites enable people to share music they create or enjoy. These sites often allow people to create playlists from songs they like and see what music their friends on the site are listening to and sharing. *Example:* www.spotify.com.

Presentation and document-sharing sites

These websites enable people to share whitepapers, presentations, articles, or other content they've created. *Example:* www.scribd.com.

Live-streaming sites

Live-streaming platforms help individuals and companies share live video with the world. *Example:* www.livestream.com.

Networking Services

Networking services exist to help connect like-minded people. These sites make it possible for people to easily share thoughts or ideas, contribute to a cause, collaborate on projects, and learn about topics they're interested in. Here are examples of social media networking services.

Social networking sites

Social networking sites (also called social networks) bring people of similar interests together. While the terms *social media, social networking,* and *social networks* are often used interchangeably, they actually have different meanings. Boyd and Ellison (2007) define these social networks as "web-based services that allow individuals to (1) construct a public or semi-public profile within a bounded system, (2) articulate a list of other users with whom they share a connection, and (3) view and traverse their list of connections and those made by others within the system. The nature and nomenclature of these connections may vary from site to site" (unpaged). *Example:* The most popular example of these is, of course, www.Facebook.com.

Microblogging on real-time platforms

According to Mark Glaser (2007), Executive Editor of PBS Mediashift, microblogging enables people to "write brief text updates about your life on the go, and send them to friends and interested observers via text messaging, instant messaging, email or the web" (unpaged). *Example:* One popular real-time platform limits people to just 140 characters, www.twitter.com.

Opinion and review sites

These sites enable people to share their opinions or reviews of products and services. In many cases, companies incorporate this functionality into their own sites, so their customers can review products and people can see these authentic reviews directly on the company's website. *Example:* www.amazon.com.

Social shopping sites

Social shopping sites give members limited-time or exclusive group deals and discounts. Sometimes the offers are limited to a certain number of buyers; other times, they are only activated if enough people commit to purchasing an item or service. *Example:* http://www.groupon.com.

Crowdsourcing sites

According to Jeff Howe (n.d.), a contributing editor for *Wired* magazine, crowdsourcing is "the act of taking a job traditionally performed by a designated agent (usually an employee) and outsourcing it to an undefined, generally large group of people in the form of an open call" (unpaged). Crowdsourcing websites and platforms bring people together to contribute ideas and actions and achieve a common goal. Some brands, such as Starbucks, have even built their own crowdsourcing sites to obtain ideas from their customers and improve their businesses. *Example:* http://mystarbucksidea.force.com.

As you can see, there is a lot of overlap with the various social media services. For example, Facebook is a platform that enables video- and photo-sharing, blogging, real-time updates, and other components of social media. YouTube is a video-sharing site but also a community and social networking site.

Many of these platforms have mobile components that allow consumers to access them easily via their smartphones and mobile devices. With technology changing so rapidly, platforms that further combine mobile and social technologies will continue to develop—for example, in the location-sharing category. These platforms, such as Foursquare and Banjo, utilize GPS functionality to allow users to "check in" at places and share their locations with their friends. Businesses may even reward people for sharing their location and checking in with them for exclusive discounts and coupons.

The key thing to remember is that social media tools and platforms have given the average person the ability to share his or her voice, opinions, and content with the world and for others to comment on and join in on conversations about this content. And, importantly, consumers have access to this online content at all times—it does not close at 5 p.m.

THE BACKGROUND AND RISE OF SOCIAL MEDIA

*I*n order to understand the cultural and business significance of social media, it's important to examine how we arrived at this point.

In the past, communication and collaboration between individuals or groups of people could be difficult and/or expensive. Individuals or groups wanting to share opinions with the world, influence others, or market products and services could choose from only a few outlets: print media, radio, and TV.

During the 1990s, online tools and technology began to enable large numbers of people to share their opinions and communicate with others. Dating sites and message boards were some of the early platforms that enabled open communication and dialogue, and in 1997 Six Degrees was launched as the first "modern" social network that enabled users to create a profile and become friends with other people.

In 1999, Livejournal inspired a different breed of platforms— blogs—that enabled people to share their thoughts online and write whatever they wanted. Blogs have changed the nature of publishing, as people no longer need technical knowledge or large sums of money to publish their thoughts and opinions. By early 2012 the Internet housed over 180 million blogs (Nielsen, 2012).

With the launch of Friendster in 2002, social networking continued to evolve, allowing people to easily connect with friends and friends of friends online. MySpace, which allowed users to customize the look and feel of their profiles, launched in 2003 and became the most popular social network by 2006. However, by 2008, Facebook, which initially launched in 2004 as a social network for college students, surpassed MySpace to become the world's most popular social network. By March 2012, Facebook had over 900 million active users worldwide (Facebook, n.d.).

In 2005, YouTube launched as a site that allowed people to easily upload, share, and engage with videos. It's still the largest site of its kind; each minute over 60 hours of video are uploaded to YouTube (n.d.).

Along the way, people have become empowered to share their opinions and ideas, create content, share content, meet new people, and consume vast amounts of information. The online platform in all its manifestations has completely changed the way people search for products, find information, communicate with, interact with, and experience the world.

SOCIAL MEDIA'S IMPACT ON PEOPLE

 et's look at how people are actually using social media and how social media tools and platforms impact our lives.

Who Is Using Social Media?

ComScore (2012) reports that almost one out of every five minutes spent online is currently being spent on social networking sites. According to a 2011 report from the Pew Research Center's Internet & American Life Project (Hampton, Goulet, Rainie, & Purcell, 2011), nearly half of adults (47 percent), or 59 percent of Internet users, say they use at least one social networking service. This is almost double the 26 percent of adults (34 percent of Internet users) who reported using a social networking site in 2008. A 2011 study from Nielsen (2011) reports that even more people are using social media websites and platforms. The study found that almost four out of five active Internet users visit social networks and blogs.

Another key finding from the Pew Research Center's report is that the average age of the social media user is getting older. The average age increased from 33 in 2008 to 38 in 2010, and over half of social media users are over 35 years old. Exhibit 1.2 shows the age breakdown of social networking site users in 2008 and 2010, according to the Pew Research Center.

EXHIBIT 1.2   Age distribution of social networking site users in 2008 and 2010.

Percent of social networking site users in each age group. For instance, in 2008, 28% of social networking site users were 18–22, but in 2010 that age group made up 16% of social networking site users.

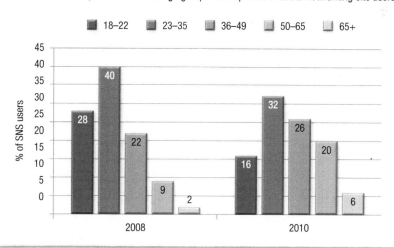

Source: Pew Research Center's Internet & American Life Social Network Site survey conducted on landline and cell phone between October 20 and November 28, 2010. N for full sample is 2,255 and margin of error is +/– 2.3 percentage points. N for social network site and Twitter users is 975 and margin of error is +/– 3.5 percentage points. Used with permission.

Lastly, the Pew Research Center's findings show that more females than males use social networking services (56 percent female vs. 44 percent male). Women also comprise the majority of email users, bloggers, and those who use a photo-sharing service. On the other hand, more males than females (61 vs. 39 percent) are considered "power sharers" (see the discussion of Exhibit 1.3).

How Do People Use Social Media?

Social media allows participation in a great variety of activities. Below we list a few ways that people are using social media in their lives.

Keeping up with friends

A recent study from IBM's Institute for Business Value confirms what we might have guessed: 70 percent of people visit social media sites to connect with their friends and family (IBM Global Business Services, n.d.). According to the Pew Research Center's Internet & American Life Project, people are increasingly using social media services to maintain contact with their close friends and family. Approximately 40 percent of all social networking users have friended their closest confidants, an 11 percent increase from 2008.

Assisting with and talking about purchase decisions

People are increasingly using social media content to help them make better purchasing decisions. According to a report from ROI Research, 59 percent of active social network users use these networks to compare prices; 56 percent who do so talk about sales or specials (Performics, 2011). The study also reported that 32 percent of users said that they had made a sports-related product purchase because of something they saw that was posted on a social network.

Access news and entertainment

According to the study from IBM's Institute for Business Value, just under half of consumers who visit social networking sites do so for the purpose of accessing news (49 percent) or entertainment (46 percent). As we'll explore later in this textbook, this is definitely something that sport marketers should take advantage of.

Sharing information and accessing reviews

Many people aren't shy about expressing their opinions and ideas on social media websites, and many also use these sites to access others' reviews. According to IBM, 42 percent of social media users go to social media sites to share their opinions. A 2011 study from Yahoo! and Added Value found that 56 percent of social networking users are "power sharers" and share information on a daily basis or even more frequently (Yahoo! Advertising Solutions, 2011). See Exhibit 1.3 for a profile of these power sharers according to this study.

Reviews are becoming increasingly important. The IBM survey referenced earlier found that 39 percent of people use social media sites to access product reviews. According to a 2011 study from Cone, Inc., 87 percent of shoppers said positive reviews helped them confirm their decision to purchase, while 80 percent of respondents said that reading a negative review made them change their mind about a potential purchase (Mahoney, 2011).

Interacting with companies

A significant number of people interact with brands and companies on social media websites. The study from IBM's Institute for Business Value

EXHIBIT 1.3   Profile of power sharers on social networks.

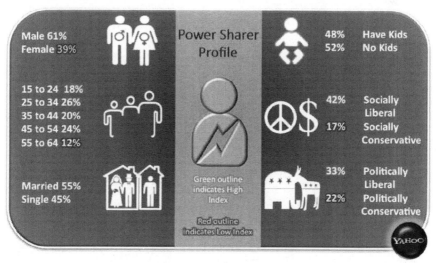

Male 61%		Power Sharer Profile		48%	Have Kids
Female 39%				52%	No Kids
15 to 24 18%					
25 to 34 26%				42%	Socially Liberal
35 to 44 20%					
45 to 54 24%				17%	Socially Conservative
55 to 64 12%					
		Green outline indicates High Index		33%	Politically Liberal
Married 55%					
Single 45%		Red outline indicates Low Index		22%	Politically Conservative

Source: Yahoo! Advertising Solutions (2011). Used with permission.

Using social media to find a job

Social media can have an impact on your job search and career. With blogs, forums, content-sharing sites, and other social networks, it's possible to find others who are hiring (or who have a career that you are considering) and network with them. You can also use your blog and presence on social networking sites to showcase your expertise in a given topic or field and be recognized for your knowledge.

Here's a real-world story of how social media helped someone land a job. In early 2010, Laura Gainor (currently a social media manager for GMR Marketing) and her husband moved from Charlotte, North Carolina, to Milwaukee, Wisconsin. Before they moved, she decided to apply for a job she had seen posted February 11 at Comet Branding, a social media and communications agency. Laura demonstrated her creativity and passion for the job by creating a poster with the Comet logo on it and a hashtag—the symbol "#" used to indicate keywords in a tweet—called #LauraGainorToMilwaukee. She kicked off her job-seeking campaign by posting a video to Twitter. As she and her husband traveled across the United States to look for a house, she took pictures of herself with the Comet Branding poster in a variety of locations. She posted the pictures online, checked in to various places with Foursquare, and contacted Comet Branding on Twitter to let them know what she was doing.

After returning home, Laura created a presentation that described what she had done. She posted the presentation to the document-sharing website, Slideshare. Within 36 hours the Slideshare presentation had been viewed over 1,000 times (Gainor, 2010). Fewer than 10 days after the presentation was posted, Laura obtained an interview with Comet Branding founders Al Krueger and Sara Meaney through Skype, a platform that enables people to make free calls through the Internet. She then had an in-person interview on March 1 when she arrived in Milwaukee and was offered the job on the spot.

As you can see, it is definitely possible to utilize social media to help yourself stand out to potential employers in order to obtain your dream job.

found that 23 percent of social networking users listed interacting with brands as a reason why they visit social networking sites, and 45 percent of people said they interact with brands on social networking sites (IBM Global Business Services, n.d.). The Nielsen study (2011) reported that 53 percent of active adult social networkers follow a brand, while 32 percent follow a celebrity. According to the IBM study, the top reasons people gave for interacting with brands on social media sites were:

- Gain access to a discount (61 percent)
- Purchase a product (55 percent)

- See reviews and product rankings (53 percent)
- Get access to general information (53 percent)
- Get access to exclusive information (52 percent)
- Learn about new products (51 percent)

Interestingly, some of the least popular reasons why people interact with companies on social media sites were to feel connected, submit ideas for new products/services, and be part of a community. This data shows that people are typically looking for tangible value from brands they follow online.

So how does social media affect sport fans? We'll be exploring this throughout the rest of the book, but here's one example. Imagine for a moment that you're a fan of the NFL's Indianapolis Colts. In the past you would have had to read a newspaper, watch TV news, or read an article about the team on the team's website to get information about them. Now there are countless ways to follow the team, express your opinions, and connect with other Colts fans all over the world. For example, you can follow the team on Facebook and join the team's official online community, www.colts.com.fanzone.

On Facebook (http://www.facebook.com/colts) the Colts post a variety of content, ranging from links to stories about the team to videos of press conferences and game highlights. They also feature contests and sweepstakes for fans to participate in. On the MyColts.net community, fans can join the site, create a profile, connect with other fans, and read and contribute to discussions about the team. There is also a points system that rewards fans for their participation. These are just two examples of how social media outlets have further enabled fans to follow their favorite teams.

SOCIAL MEDIA'S IMPACT ON COMPANIES

As is readily apparent, companies are also using social media in ever-expanding and creative ways. In this section, we'll look at how companies are using and investing in social media, as well as why they've adopted social media tools and technologies.

Basic Information on Companies and Social Media

More companies are beginning to invest in social media, and the companies currently investing in it anticipate increasing their investments in the near future. The CMO Survey from August 2011 (Privett, 2011) found that marketers plan to increase their level of spending on social media from the current average of 7 percent of their overall marketing budgets to 10 percent over the next year. This number is up from 3.5 percent in August 2009. Christine Moorman, director of the study, says that "social media is fast becoming an important strategic weapon in company arsenals and has proven to be a valuable tool in acquiring and engaging customers."

According to a Burson-Marsteller study (2012), 87 of the largest 100 companies in the Fortune Global 500 index are using at least one social media platform. Here is the breakdown of the most popular platforms being utilized by Fortune 100 companies:

- Twitter: 82 percent
- YouTube: 79 percent
- Facebook: 74 percent
- Google+: 48 percent

Interestingly, these companies are not just creating one account on these services. These companies have on average over ten accounts each on Facebook and Twitter and eight accounts on YouTube. As we'll discuss later, sport marketers can take advantage of many opportunities by using such technologies and tools.

The companies surveyed in the Burson-Marsteller study are not just creating a presence on these social media sites; they're actively using them. For example, the study found that 93 percent of companies with Facebook pages had posted an update in the previous week.

One challenge that companies face with social media is integrating it into their overall business and marketing strategies. According to the CMO Survey (Privett, 2011), 22 percent of companies reported that social media is "not integrated at all" with their overall business strategy, and 17 percent said social media is "not integrated at all" with their marketing strategy. From a sport marketing perspective, we hope some of the strategies and best practices that we'll outline in this book will help marketers improve the way they integrate social media, especially in how they market to and communicate with fans.

How Companies Use Social Media

According to the 2011 Social Media Marketing Industry Report (Stelzner, 2011), 90 percent of marketers surveyed said that social media is important for their business. Let's look at how companies are using social media and discuss some of the benefits.

Generating additional awareness and exposure

Social media provides many opportunities for businesses to reach people and expose them to their brand, products, services, and content. Of the marketers surveyed in the Social Media Marketing Industry Report (Stelzner, 2011), 88 percent reported that generating more business exposure was a benefit of social media marketing. Just like in the traditional media world, where marketers aim to expose people to their ads multiple times in their attempt to remain visible, social media provides increased reach and frequency for marketers. However, instead of just blasting people with messages through social media channels, the smart marketers engage in conversations with people about topics they care about.

Enhanced customer service

Another reason social media is being utilized by companies is to provide customer service to people in new ways. According to a survey of Fortune 1000 executives, 52 percent of executives reported that their companies use social media for customer service (Capgemini, 2011). The real-time nature of many social media platforms and websites means that companies can often answer people's questions quickly and efficiently. This can help companies save money on call center costs and make it easier for companies to help people with their questions.

Driving website traffic and subscribers

When businesses post links on social media websites, this helps drive traffic back to their websites. The 2011 Social Media Marketing Industry Report indicates that 72 percent of marketers feel that increased traffic and subscribers is a benefit of marketing through social media. The study also found that 62 percent of marketers said improved search rankings are a benefit of social media marketing. We'll talk more about the intersection of search marketing and social media in Chapter 6.

Improved research and monitoring

Social media and related tools allow people to easily connect around common interests, form bonds, and make their opinions heard. People talk about brands they love and hate on social media sites. This is a potential goldmine for businesses to understand what people are saying about their products, services, and competitors. For example, a company such as Gold's Gym can monitor a site like Twitter to see what people like and don't like about their gym and member services and make changes based on their findings. The ability to get unfiltered, real-time feedback from people online can help companies make better decisions in their marketing and product development efforts. This research can also help supplement (or maybe replace) traditional focus groups.

Generating leads and improving sales

A final major benefit of social media is that companies can utilize social media websites and tools to help increase leads and sales. For example, a company can post a link on Twitter announcing a special sale and an exclusive discount code and see how many people purchase or sign up to receive more information as a result of this post. According to the 2011 Social Media Marketing Industry Report, 51 percent of marketers reported that social media marketing helped generate qualified leads, and 43 percent said it increased sales.

How Social Media Impacts the Media

As we've seen, social media has had great impact on businesses of all types, but traditional media companies have been among the most affected. In the past, media companies had almost complete control over news gathering and reporting. In order for companies and individuals to get coverage, they had to go through the media; in order for people to find out about a breaking story, they had to hear it from the media.

Due to the rise of blogs, message boards, real-time information sharing, and other social tools, people now get their news from many sources. This has had a huge impact on breaking news. In the sport world, for example, major stories are often broken via Twitter and other social media outlets, sometimes to the dismay of owners and general managers. As a growing number of companies and individuals have access to content creation tools, everyone has the opportunity to become a publisher and a potential breaker of news.

Media companies also benefit from social media, of course. Today, reporters are able to use social media outlets as sources for inspiration, research, documentation, and promotion. Reporters can easily seek opinions about what is important to people and may seek input and information for a particular story. Later, we'll discuss crowd-sourcing and other ways media and the public work together to form news coverage.

How Companies Are Measuring Social Media

Marketers use a variety of metrics in trying to estimate and understand the value of social media and its impact on their organizations. As reported in eMarketer (2011), according to the August 2011 CMO Survey, the most popular metrics are website traffic numbers (hits, visits, and pages views), repeat visits, and number of followers or friends on social media websites. We've devoted the final chapter of this textbook to measuring the effectiveness of social media, but Exhibit 1.4 introduces the types of metrics organizations are currently using.

EXHIBIT 1.4   Social media metrics used by U.S. marketers, August 2010 and August 2011.

% OF RESPONDENTS	AUG 2010	AUG 2011
Hits/visits/page views	47.6%	52.2%
Repeat visits	34.7%	34.9%
Number of followers or friends	24.0%	34.1%
Conversion rates (from visitor to buyer)	25.4%	29.3%
Buzz indicators (web mentions)	15.7%	20.5%
Customer acquisition costs	11.8%	14.1%
Sales levels	17.9%	13.3%
Other text analysis ratings	6.6%	12.0%
Online product/service ratings	8.2%	10.4%
Revenue per customer	17.2%	9.6%
Net promoter score	7.5%	6.8%
Customer retention costs	7.7%	6.4%
Abandoned shopping carts	3.8%	4.8%
Profits per customer	9.4%	4.8%

Source: Data from Duke University's Fuqua School of Business, "The CMO Survey," commissioned by the American Marketing Association (AMA), Sept. 6, 2011.

POTENTIAL NEGATIVE EFFECTS OF SOCIAL MEDIA

While social media has many overwhelmingly positive benefits for individuals and marketers, and these positives definitely outweigh the negatives, we would be remiss not to cover a few of its potential negative effects. It's important that you, as sport marketers and business professionals, are aware of all the potential effects of social media.

Exposes Brands and People to Criticism

In the past, brands had most of the control when it came to communicating with their audiences through the media. With social tools such as blogs, podcasts, videos, and online communities, people now have more power when it comes to voicing their opinions online. In the past, people may have criticized a brand by telling a friend or group of friends in person, or through an email. Now, many people's comments and criticisms are public on social networks and have the ability to be seen by thousands or millions of people. Negative comments and criticisms can directly impact an individual or organization's reputation and hurt his or her image or business.

Potential Damage to Employees' Companies and Careers

While social media can be very helpful in finding a job, it can also have a negative effect on your career if you're not careful. According to Frazier (2010), in May 2010, Ashley Johnson, a waitress at Brixx Pizza in Charlotte, North Carolina, was upset when she received what she thought was a poor tip from a group she had waited on. She later posted on Facebook, "Thanks for eating at Brixx, you cheap piece of _____ camper."

It turns out that her post violated two company policies:

1. The policy against speaking disparagingly about customers.
2. The policy against casting the restaurant in a negative light on social networks.

A few days later, the managers at Brixx showed her a copy of her comment and fired her. Thus, this illustrates how social media content, used irresponsibly, can damage employees' companies and their careers. The lesson here is to use good judgment when posting your thoughts and opinions online. Know your company's policies and realize that everything you say online is essentially public.

Potential to Be Used for Destructive Behavior

For all the good actions that people and companies engage through social media, people also may use these tools to engage in destructive behavior. One example of this is the phenomenon of flash mob robberies. Flash mobs originally began as spontaneous gatherings of people who would dance or perform together. However, flash mobs have also been organized to commit crimes, such as robberies. In these cases, websites such as Facebook and Twitter have been used to bring a group of people together in order to orchestrate a robbery. Police say that suspects typically select a time and location to rob and discuss what they want to take in order to escape without being caught. For all the good in social media, it's unfortunate that some people misuse these tools to engage in illegal activity.

Free Speech and Communication Issues

New forms of communication often result in attempts to restrict its use. In some cases, employers have banned the use of social media on certain days or certain times of day. For example, the NHL's social media policy aims to prevent players from using social media beginning two hours prior to face-off on game days and extending until after players have finished their post game media obligations (Dillman, 2011).

In other cases, organizations have gone even further in banning social media use by potentially restricting employees' freedom of speech. In Missouri, part of the Amy Hestir Student Protection Act prevents teachers from interacting with students on non-work-related social media sites unless the conversation is fully public (Heaton, 2011). This basically makes it illegal for teachers and students to use online chat services, which can be helpful in giving students a means to ask questions that they might not have asked during class. As of this writing, the Missouri State Teachers Association is seeking an injunction against this particular section of the law. It will be interesting to watch how free speech on social media sites is regulated and protected over the next few years.

Athletic Recruiting Loopholes and Violations

Many rules regarding the recruitment of athletes were created before many forms of social media even existed. Coupled with the fact that social media changes constantly, a gray area has emerged. For example, the NCAA has many rules that regulate when coaches can contact high school athletes and how many times they're allowed to contact them. In some cases coaches may not be able to call or text a prospect, but they may be able to send him or her a Facebook or Twitter message (Hooker, 2011). This type of contact may be helpful or it may be annoying to prospects and even interfere with their daily lives. And it may violate the spirit of NCAA restrictions even if it's technically not prohibited.

CONCLUSION

Ultimately, social media has changed the way we experience the world. Communication and collaboration are easier, faster, and, in many ways, better. Understanding the basics of social media and how new websites, tools, and technologies are affecting consumers and organizations is vital to understanding social media's impact on sport and the ways sport marketers can take advantage of this. You should now have a solid base of knowledge about social media to draw from as we explore more about how social media is affecting sport marketing.

REVIEW QUESTIONS

1. In your own words, what is social media?
2. What are three ways people use social media?
3. Give a couple examples of how social media is affecting businesses. In what way do you think social media has affected companies the most?
4. What do you think is the most important negative aspect of social media that marketers should be concerned with? The most positive?

REFERENCES

Boyd, D. M., & Ellison, N. B. (2007). Social network sites: Definition, history, and scholarship. *Journal of Computer-Mediated Communication, 13*(1), article 11. Retrieved from http://jcmc.indiana.edu/vol13/issue1/boyd.ellison.html.

Burson-Marsteller (2010, February 23). Burson-Marsteller Fortune Global 100 social media study. Retrieved from http://www.burson-marsteller.com/Innovation_and_insights/blogs_and_podcasts/BM_Blog/Lists/Posts/Post.aspx?ID=160.

Burson-Marsteller (2012, June 15). Burson-Marsteller global social media check up 2012. Retrieved from http://www.slideshare.net/BMGlobalNews/b-m-global-social-media-checkup-2012-deck-13341217.

Capgemini (2011, July 25). Executive outsourcing survey. Retrieved from Business Wire website http://www.istockanalyst.com/business/news/5311010/capgemini-survey-reveals-the-rising-importance-of-social-media-to-customer-care.

ComScore (2012, Jan. 4). It's a social world: Top 10 need-to-knows about social networking and where it's headed. Retrieved from http://www.comscore.com/Press_Events/Presentations_Whitepapers/2011/it_is_a_social_world_top_10_need-to-knows_about_social_networking.

Dillman, L. (2011, September 15). NHL's new social media policy includes black-outs on game days. *Los Angeles Times*. Retrieved from http://latimesblogs.latimes.com/sports_blog/2011/09/nhl-social-networking-tweeting-nba.html.

Dresher, B. (2010, August 6). USA Today: More than just news. A social media case study. Retrieved from http://www.slideshare.net/YNPNdc/usa-today-more-than-just-news-a-social-media-case-study.

eMarketer (2011, September 15). As social spending rises, which methods are CMOs focusing on? Retrieved from http://www.emarketer.com/Article.aspx?R=1008591.

Facebook (n.d.). Key facts. Retrieved from http://newsroom.fb.com/content/default.aspx?NewsAreaId=22.

Frazier, E. (2010, May 17). Facebook post cost waitress her job: Online gripe is like standing on a corner with a sign, lawyer says. *Charlotte Observer*. Retrieved from http://www.charlotteobserver.com/2010/05/17/1440447/facebook-post-costs-waitress-her.html.

Gainor, L. (2010, March 10). Laura Gainor utilizing social media = Hired at Comet Branding. Retrieved from http://cometbranding.com/blog/laura-gainor-utilizing-social-media-hired-at-comet-branding.

Glaser, M. (2007, May 15). Your guide to micro-blogging and Twitter. Retrieved from http://www.pbs.org/mediashift/2007/05/your-guide-to-micro-blogging-and-twitter135.html.

Griner, D. (2009, September 01). Everything you need to know about social media. Retrieved from http://www.slideshare.net/Griner/everything-you-need-to-know-about-social-media-1937744.

Hampton, K., Sessions Goulet, L., Rainie, L., & Purcell, K. (2011). Social networking sites and our lives. *Pew Internet and American Life Project*. Retrieved from http://www.pewinternet.org/Reports/2011/Technology-and-social-networks.aspx.

Heaton, B. (2011, August 22). Missouri teachers sue over social media restrictions. Retrieved from http://www.govtech.com/education/Missouri-Teachers-Sue-Over-Social-Media-Restrictions.html.

Hooker, D. (2011, August 17). Social media is way to beat the system. Retrieved from http://espn.go.com/college-sports/recruiting/football/story/_/id/6871086/social-media-allows-loopholes-ncaa-rules.

Howe, J. (n.d.). Crowdsourcing: A definition. Retrieved from http://crowd sourcing.typepad.com/.

IBM Global Business Services (n. d.). From social media to social CRM: What customers want the first in a two-part series. Retrieved from http://www. slideshare.net/duckofdoom/ibm-why-people-follow-brands.

Mahoney, S. (2011, August 31). Study: Negative reviews grow more powerful. *Marketing Daily*. Retrieved from http://www.mediapost.com/publications/ article/157679/.

Nielsen (2009, March 9). Social networking's new global footprint. Retrieved from http://blog.nielsen.com/nielsenwire/global/social-networking-new- global-footprint/.

Nielsen (2011). State of the media: The social media report. Retrieved from http://blog.nielsen.com/nielsenwire/social/.

Nielsen (2012, March 8). Buzz in the blogosphere: Millions more bloggers and blog readers. Retrieved from http://blog.nielsen.com/nielsenwire/online_ mobile/buzz-in-the-blogosphere-millions-more-bloggers-and-blog-readers/.

Performics (2011, June 7). New social media study: Nearly 60 percent say Linked-In is most important social network account. Retrieved from http://blog. performics.com/search/2011/06/new-social-media-study-nearly-60-percent- say-linkedin-is-most-important-social-network-account.html.

Privett, C. (2011). CMO survey marketers to significantly increase their invest- ment. Retrieved from http://www.fuqua.duke.edu/news_events/releases/ cmo-survey-sep-11.

Safko, L., & Brake, D. K. (2009). *The social media bible: Tactics, tools and strategies for business success.* New York: Wiley, 2009.

Stelzner, M. (2011, April 7). 2011 social media marketing industry report. Retrieved from http://www.socialmediaexaminer.com/social-media- marketing-industry-report-2011/.

Thornley, J. (2008, August 08). What is "social media"? Retrieved from http:// propr.ca/2008/what-is-social-media/.

Yahoo! Advertising Solutions (2011, August 3). Infographic: Who shares the most on social networks. Retrieved from http://archive.feedblitz.com/ 669264/~4052540.

YouTube (n. d.). Statistics. Retrieved from http://www.youtube.com/t/press_ statistics.

Introduction to Principles of Sport Communication, Marketing, and Social Media

INTRODUCTION

S port touches people's lives in unique ways, so it should come as no surprise that communicating about and marketing sport through social media also require unique approaches. Robert Tuchman, author of *The 100 Sporting Events You Must See Live: An Insider's Guide to Creating the Sports Experience of a Lifetime,* writes about the unique ability of sport to bring people together: "There is no greater camaraderie than sitting in a section of fans that bleed the same team colors . . . cultural differences become meaningless . . . there are no differences in ethnicity, income level, or age . . . we are united in cheering, jeering, and just enjoying the sporting event" (Tuchman, 2009, pp. 1–3).

Sport consumption is a special form of consumption distinguished by both the intensity of emotions and by the heightened level of self-definition found among followers. Kahle and Close (2011) describe the association many fans feel toward the teams they support, combined with sport's inherently competitive nature, that meld to produce strong emotions among fans. As ESPN's Kieran Darcy once said, "For a sports fan, visiting Notre

Dame for a football weekend is like a pilgrimage, like going to Lourdes, or Jerusalem, or Mecca and Medina" (Kahle & Close, p. 132).

Beyond the social and emotional aspects, sport is a unique product because:

- Each game, match, or competition has its own outcome. Since the outcome of a sporting event is not known ahead of time, people cannot control the product.
- Although people tend to support winning teams and retract from losing teams, demand fluctuates throughout the season.
- There are intangible, ephemeral, and subjective aspects of sports, which make events very personal in nature.
- Since there are no "inventories" of games or tickets after-the-fact, sports are considered very perishable. Once the game or event is over, the focus moves to the next game or event, and, in many cases, people are left only with a memory.
- Sport organizations often compete against each other in some ways while cooperating in other ways.
- Sport is often consumed at the very same time it is produced.

Sport as an agent for bringing people together and as a unique product means that it is an industry where social media can have a dramatic impact on communication and marketing. The use of social media as marketing and communication tools opens up new types of personal communication between the organization and the consumer. Whether it is individuals re-tweeting athletes' tweets or teams communicating via posts on blogs, in the era of social media it is incumbent upon sport managers to understand the technology and its resulting impact.

According to Joe Favorito (2011), a strategic communications consultant, ideal candidates for social media positions have extraordinary communication skills (in both the online and traditional environments), speak a second language, understand the global environment, are charismatic in nature, are team players, and are capable of communicating the company's values to a global audience as well as contributing new ideas to enhance the brand of the sport organization.

EVOLUTION OF SPORT COMMUNICATION

As the mainstream media has changed, so too has the sport media. Schultz, Caskey, and Esherick (2010) say there has been a shift from sport media, "controlling production and distribution of content; deciding the what, when, and where of audience consumption" to media "fueled by new technology and defined by interactivity, audience fragmentation and empowerment, and instantaneous access" (p. 1). Let's look at how we got from a top-down model of communication to a more shared one.

The Old Model of Sport Communication

Although there is no exact moment cited as the beginning of mass media coverage of sport, 1849 marked the first telegraph coverage of championship boxing (Sowell, 2008). Match coverage, combined with the historical events surrounding industrialization, urbanization, and the growth of education, date the old model of communication all the way back to the 1850s (Schultz, Caskey, & Esherick, 2010).

In this communication model, the "media" referred first to newspapers and magazines, and then radio and television; these were the only viable means of accessing the athletes, games, events, and news related to sport. Content and publicity, including news about athletes, sport organizations, events, and games, were distributed to mass audiences exclusively via media outlets. Feedback from the audience to the media was limited, and no feedback went directly from the audience to sport organizations. Media controlled the flow of all information, meaning they were in charge of *setting the agenda*. This enabled the media to exert a significant influence on public perception through the control, filtering, and shaping of media content (McCombs & Shaw, 1972). During this early period of coverage by the mass media, sport and the media benefited financially from the arrangement. Negative stories were less likely to surface. Athletes and events received necessary publicity to promote economic growth. As sport gained popularity, content and distribution rights became more valuable, and the fees for the distribution of sporting events and products skyrocketed. Money increased the economic power and prestige of sports (both individuals and organizations). In addition, reporters and athletes developed lasting friendships and relationships that impacted the flow of information to the public in both positive and negative ways (Schultz, Caskey, & Esherick, 2010).

The New Model of Sport Communication (1990s–Present)

The traditional communication model in which the media had a monopoly and could dictate the what, when, and how of distributing sport began to change when Home Box Office (HBO) began airing boxing matches in the 1970s. This was followed by satellite programming that allowed people to watch games live without waiting for the taped versions of the events to be shown on their local stations (Federal Communications Commission, 2005).

The technologies of home computers, Internet, satellite television, and digital transmissions created two immediate impacts for sport communication: (1) the power of traditional mass media decreased as fans benefited from multiple consumption options, such as live streaming and satellite radio, and (2) the sport audience became empowered as never before to consume sporting events as they desired instead of only as made available by the media (Schultz, Caskey, & Esherick, 2010). In fact, social media has expanded the "coverage" of sport to all the time as people talk about teams, players, and organizations twenty-four hours a day, seven days a week. Professionals in the field of sport must understand that they always, at all hours of the day, represent the organization they work for and that the personal/professional line cannot easily be separated in the global arena of social media (Favorito, 2011).

Perhaps the most important effect of these technologies, however, has been greater audience empowerment: Individuals use technologies to become actual participants in the sport communication process. Furthermore, fans have started to challenge the mainstream media by creating and distributing content independent from them. Through the use of social media and the Internet, individuals are able to create and comment on content in the world of sport at any time. When a story emerges (or sometimes is even unconfirmed), people post messages on blogs, Twitter, or message boards. These stories quickly gain traction without being published in a mainstream news outlet. Even major news outlets and television shows are now using social media to take polls and gather comments about stories to show on the bottom of the screen to enable greater levels of participation amongst viewers.

As Exhibit 2.1 illustrates, the coverage of a sport story in the modern communication model depends upon the intricate flow between the media and audience. According to sport media professionals at Sports Media Challenge (SMC), the shift has gone from a time when communication/marketing professionals would put out materials based upon what they wanted to discuss or what they felt the public wanted to hear to now, when it is more of "a conversation, where the fans get to say what they want to talk about and get to direct where the marketing focus needs to be" (Garner, Patrick, Barrett, & Lane, 2010). In fact, this is idea is further illustrated in Exhibit 2.2, with Brian Solis depicting the various cogs in the social consumer machine.

EXHIBIT 2.1 Coverage of a sports story in modern communication model.

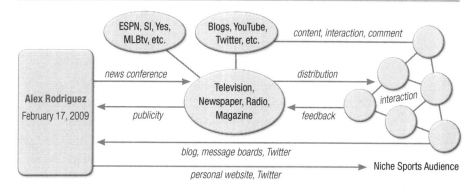

Source: Schultz, B., Caskey, P. H., & Esherick, C. (2010). *Media relations in sport* (3rd ed.). Morgantown, WV: Fitness Information Technology, p. 19, Figure 1.4. Used with permisssion.

EXHIBIT 2.2 The roles of the social consumer.

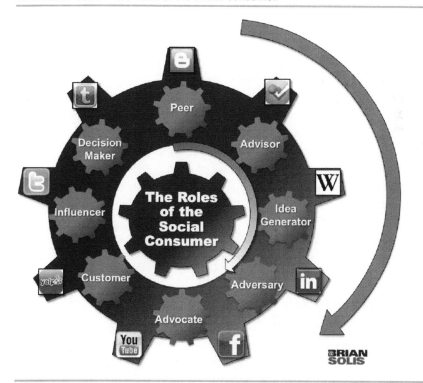

Source: Brian Solis, The roles of the social consumer (2010, Dec. 29). Retrieved from http://www.flickr.com/photos/briansolis/5303340481.

How social media has intensified the need for crisis management—and made it easier

The ever-increasing access to news and information has intensified the need for sport organizations to deal with crisis situations through a variety of media outlets, including social media. Whether a sudden crisis occurs or an ongoing issue continues for months despite the best efforts of management, the organization must address the situation; it cannot be ignored. It does not matter if the issue involves a player's off-field behavior or customer complaints with far-reaching implications; the best advice for all crisis situations is to respond quickly. Regardless of the crisis or the method selected to communicate with the public, sport professionals should avoid obfuscating the issues. Furthermore, retaliation and pontification both tend to increase the tensions and delay resolution. Confrontations and lawsuits should be avoided, if possible, because they keep controversies in the forefront of the public's consciousness. The best course of action is to provide a consistent message via all appropriate channels in both the social media arena as well as traditional news outlets. Take advantage of the ability to provide accurate and timely information, especially since social media creates an effective way of distributing messages to interested parties.

In addition, organizations need to be proactive in closely monitoring their athletes, coaches, and employees to stay on top of emerging stories. There really is no excuse for a complete surprise when information is brewing in the press or social media. In fact, many types of online tools exist to help monitor your brand, including Google Alerts, a service that allows you to receive notifications if new search queries related to words or phrases of your choosing appear on Google. If negative postings are hurting your company's image, address it with polite, corrective statements and appropriate comments. Use your official blog, website, and other social media outlets to convey the correct information. Furthermore, have policies and procedures in place ahead of time that outline how your organization will handle crisis situations. This includes knowing who the company spokesperson is in the event of an emergency, training key personnel on crisis management, anticipating potential problems, and developing specific plans to handle a crisis situation. Be prepared!

THE CHANGING LANDSCAPE OF SPORT MARKETING

Not only has social media affected sport communication, it has also impacted the marketing of sport. While definitions vary, most define sport marketing as "all activities designed to meet the needs and wants of sport consumers through exchange processes" (Mullin, 2007, p. 9). As this suggests, sport marketing centers on the consumer

Consumers seek ads

A search of YouTube for "NFL Sunday Ticket commercials" yields many results, posted both by DirecTV and other users not related to the company. Many of the top results have thousands of views, meaning that people actively seek out these commercials apart from seeing them on TV. This means that organizations have many ways to reach consumers other than the traditional and often expensive method of television advertising. Sport marketers can benefit greatly from creative and proactive approaches when developing media campaigns. Of course, one must never forget that while it is easy to post material online, it is almost impossible to take it down, especially if the content is controversial.

and the purchasing decisions associated with a sport organization's goods and/or services. For example, sport marketing can occur before a consumer decides to attend an event, continue through the event, and extend after the event ends. Sporting events are promoted ahead of time to build enthusiasm for the event. Promotions during and after the event are designed to encourage repeat consumption. Every aspect should be considered and planned for by the sport professional. Furthermore, the use of social media at each point should be considered to maximize the number of "personal touches" the sport consumer experiences in relation to the event.

Sport marketing includes both marketing *the* sport and marketing *through* sport. Marketing the sport focuses on the actual team, game, sport, sport service, or product. For example, organizations such as the National Football League (NFL), the National Basketball Association (NBA), and the National Collegiate Athletic Association (NCAA) have all created television commercials promoting their respective sports and teams. One NFL television advertisement from the 2010 season included the tag line, "You want the NFL, come to the NFL . . . buynfltickets.com." The advertisement promoted the sale of tickets to all 32 NFL teams, and the commercial showed a variety of sports fans, teams, and logos.

Marketing *through* sport, on the other hand, refers to using sports to promote a specific good or product. This occurs when a non–sport-related company markets themselves by aligning with a sport organization, event, or brand. For example, DirecTV created a variety of commercials that focused on the rivalry of certain NFL teams (Redskins versus Cowboys, Dolphins versus Patriots, etc.) in order to promote the NFL Sunday Ticket, which is exclusively available through DirecTV.

The growth of the social media and ongoing advances in technology have created unique, powerful, and intriguing opportunities for marketing sport and for marketing through sport, some of which are illustrated in Exhibit 2.3 (enlarge and study in detail on www.the

EXHIBIT 2.3   The Conversation Prism.

Source: Brian Solis, www.briansolis.com, and JESS3. Used with permission.

conversationprism.com). As stated previously, social media enables conversations between organizations and consumers. Organizations now have an opportunity to engage in communication, collaboration, education, and/or entertainment with customers, prospective customers, employees, and other stakeholders (people who are affected by a company's decisions in some way). Each stakeholder network has the capacity to influence its members. If that influence can be converted into a desired outcome or action, then the organization has obtained a valuable resource to be used in any marketing campaign. Keep in mind that the most powerful form of marketing is still word of mouth. As a result, it is imperative to cultivate stakeholders and use them to positively impact a marketing campaign. The next logical step is to direct these conversations, networks, and actions in such a way as to generate action on the part of each network. If people have positive experiences at an event, the next step is for them to invite friends to attend in the future; the result will be increased ticket sales over time.

Make a plan and see it through. One of the biggest mistakes sport organizations make when implementing a social media campaign is that they invest money and effort into it and expect a quick result, especially in terms of ticket sales. When the organization does not see the anticipated result quickly enough, its tendency is to switch to a different tactic. Organizations with a more long-term strategy (longer than six-month increments) generally have stronger social media campaigns and results (Favorito, 2011).

Sport organizations, especially smaller ones, usually do not have the expertise to implement a thorough campaign designed to maximize information technology; however, companies and computer software programs exist for that purpose. For example, the Chicago Fire, a major league soccer (MLS) team, uses the web-based client enablement platform offered by FIPPEX. According to the company, FIPPEX enables organizations to "gather critical intelligence, seamlessly interact with customers, and enhance . . . sales and marketing initiatives [by providing] businesses the power to move beyond passive relationship management to active communications." Read more about the benefits associated with this collaboration in the box on the next page.

Businesses and entrepreneurs are just beginning to see ways in which traditional marketing techniques may be supplemented, improved upon, and even replaced to turn social media interactions into meaningful marketing results. But underneath the new vocabulary, applications, and tools, marketing with social media should be based on time-tested fundamentals of business and marketing. Success depends upon:

1. Understanding and participating in the evolving marketplace.
2. Clearly communicating your message to the right people.
3. Assessing the effectiveness of your work.
4. Constantly revising, adapting, and updating your plans.

Marketing with social media, however, also requires transforming traditional marketing techniques to include other ways of approaching the marketing mix—relationship marketing and persuasion marketing.

How the Chicago Fire engages season ticket holders all season long

HANK STEINBRECHER
President of Touchline Consulting and Chairman of Synthetic Turf Association

"After several meetings with the Chicago Fire and members of FIPPEX it was clear the platform would enable the Fire to reach out to customers in new and innovative ways. More specifically, the system prompts the sport organization to have constant dialogue with clients and gives the franchise a wealth of information about the consumers, which in turn may be used to generate improved customer service. Let me share with you one way this has changed the way things are done in Chicago. As a premier season ticket holder, I would annually receive correspondence from the organization in the form of an invoice for the upcoming season. Now with this device it is a two-way communication. I receive a letter acknowledging me as a valued customer and am given information about a special link to the organization. Once I activate my personal link, I get a message indicating the organization knows my season ticket is up for renewal. In the message, if I click on the highlighted link up pops a video from the President of the Chicago Fire inviting me to renew. Before the first game, I get another message with a video from the coach talking about what to expect from our first opponent. After the first game, I get a message saying they hope I enjoyed the match and it includes a link to a video containing the event's wrap up by the team captain. There is even a place for me to ask questions. As a follow-up communication, I receive a message from the coach saying, you asked about this topic, here's your answer. As a high paying customer, I'm certainly more impressed by these sets of communications than by simply getting an invoice in the mail each year! This two-way communication device creates intimacy between the customer and the brand. In fact, by collecting information and creating web pages, emails, and other specific communications the Chicago Fire is able to build relationships with customers and brand loyalty in new and meaningful ways."

Source: Steinbrecher, H. Personal communication, June 7, 2011.

From the 4 P's to the 4 C's of Marketing

Traditionally, professionals have relied on the four P's of the marketing mix (product, price, place, and promotion) for making marketing decisions and preparing their marketing plans. However, these elements do not reflect the two-way communication possible through social media, which incorporates true feedback from the consumer to the business. In today's world of social networking, two-way communication has become an important part of marketing. To reflect this, University of North Carolina's Robert Lauterborn suggests a transformation of the four P's of marketing to the four C's of marketing: (1) the product becomes what the consumer wants and needs, (2) the price becomes the cost of satisfying that want or need, (3) the place becomes convenience of buying, and (4) promotion becomes communication (Lauterborn, 1990). The following discussion of the four C's shows how to transform marketing strategy planning from a focus on a one-way process to two-way communication that utilizes social media.

From product to consumer wants and needs

Too often organizations create products, groups of products, or benefits and force them to work for consumers. If there is no want or need for a product or service, however, it cannot be sold. Or, if a consumer wants only a portion of the product or service, he or she will be forced to upsize or forgo the purchase without having a way to communicate to the organization. One of the main reasons why social media is so effective is due to the two-way communication it encourages. If organizations listen to what their consumers are saying (their wants and needs), they can develop better products and services for them. According to sport marketing professionals, some of the companies that are experiencing success with social media campaigns are the ones that are truly listening to their customers, even if it is in the form of complaints formally voiced on Twitter or consumers griping via social media forums. In fact, some of the more proactive companies utilize social media specifically to improve customer service and help with product development (Garner et al., 2010). If the sport organization effectively uses the Internet and data mining for information, it can create targeted communications with fans and build brand loyalty. Although the use of computer software packages and consulting companies may be limited to those organizations willing to invest in a collaborative partnership, the ideas and concepts may be adapted and used on a smaller scale by any organization or individual willing to do some data collection.

The concept is simple. Based upon formal and informal surveys (including comments in forums and chat rooms), the sport organization can collect information about the consumers and follow-up using a variety of digital mediums. If a fan identifies his favorite player, the organization can send an email with a link to a special message from that player talking about an upcoming game and a link to buy tickets. The email can also invite him to follow the player on Twitter or like his/her official Facebook page. Subsequent posts on social media platforms can offer special prices on games, discounts on concessions, or special access to team merchandise. Alternatively, post-game surveys, emails, or polls can generate comments from fans on a myriad of topics ranging from the cleanliness of the restrooms to the entertainment provided before the game. Once the organization addresses the issues revealed in the surveys, a new opportunity exists to reach out to the consumer, share information, and invite them back again. This type of ongoing, two-way communication builds brand loyalty and creates a more positive relationship between the consumer and the organization than the old style of one-way communication (Steinbrecher, 2011).

Another example of an organization using social media to meet the wants and needs of the consumers involves fantasy leagues. In 2010, the National Football League took fantasy football to the next level. The NFL incorporated video highlights into the leagues so participants can watch actual footage as they follow their players.

From price to cost to satisfy

Price is the amount of money a consumer pays for a product or service, such as $75.00 for a ticket, $4.50 for a hot dog, or $50.00 for greens fees. The consumer's *cost to satisfy* takes into account a number of other variables such as time, distance, or other activities consumers could be doing instead of buying the product or service. While it is imperative that sport marketers keep in mind the variables that matter to consumers when creating prices, consumers must also understand the myriad of influences on sport marketers when setting prices. A delicate balance between keeping the cost high enough for the business to be viable and low enough to ensure it is not prohibitive for consumers must always be maintained.

From place to convenience to buy

Place implies a fixed location where consumers go to purchase or consume goods and/or services. In the sport industry, the place could be the stadium/arena, gym, golf course, etc. These places have specific purposes; for example, games are played in stadiums, fields, gyms, courses, or courts, so they can't be readily moved or changed to accommodate customers.

Convenience, on the other hand, focuses on the consumers' involvement in a product or service. How can we make it more convenient for them to purchase or use our product? Can we make our sport product more available to consumers at home? For example, with the introduction of the Sirius/XM Sunday Drive, listeners can pay to have access to all NFL broadcasts in their home and cars as well as on their mobile devices. Football is not the only sport to offer solutions to the place vs. convenience issue, given the channels devoted to Major League Baseball (MLB), the National Hockey League (NHL), and even college sports. In fact, Notre Dame fans can download a free app for the iPhone that features live video of all seven home games, live scoring updates, video on demand clips, Twitter updates, and blog information.

Promotion to communication

Promotion is a one-way message. The organization is telling consumers "look at what we want you to buy." Communication, however, is

The Diadora campaign

Diadora, the Italian soccer apparel company, provided a real case study situation to a group of college students as a social marketing campaign for one of their specific products. The goal of the project was to develop, create, and maintain an online social media network for one of the company's independent licensees—Golden Viking Sports, LLC.

Students created a marketing plan for the development of the social media network. Great care and planning went into the creation of the Facebook and Twitter accounts. They conducted research on Diadora's competitors, such as Reebok, Puma, Adidas, Nike, Umbro, and Under Armour, to determine which tactics would be useful in the distribution of the new accounts. They developed a plan that showcased the strengths, weaknesses, opportunities, and threats of each of the company's social media networks, with an emphasis on their distribution methods. They found that the most important tactic was making others aware of the network, because without followers you cannot distribute a successful social media marketing campaign to your target audiences. It reinforced the importance of clearly communicating your message to the right people (Wampler, Johnston, Heasley, & Newman, 2011).

interactive; it gives consumers a way to voice their thoughts, both good and bad. As stated earlier, organizations must be willing to hear the bad as well as the good.

There also needs to be multiple channels for two-way communication, including phone, email, and social media sites such as Facebook and Twitter. An example of a two-way communication model is the development of ESPN's television show *SportsNation*, where viewers vote and give their opinion on over a dozen daily topics. The show encourages viewers to interact via multiple channels such as polls, Twitter, Facebook, chat rooms, forums, archives, and even widgets.

Promotion is also now a two-way communication in a manner discussed earlier: When companies encourage consumers to create ads, offer feedback on ads, and take part in marketing campaigns in other ways, those consumers value that their voices are being heard and reflected back to them.

As sport organizations embrace Lauterborn's fourth C and shift focus to interactive communication with consumers, marketing is likely to become more effective.

Relationship Marketing

Relationship marketing was originally defined as "attracting, maintaining and enhancing customer relationships" (Berry, 1983). In a general sense, relationship marketing refers to marketing strategies that take place over time and are designed to establish and maintain a profitable, long-term relationship with a customer (Novo, n.d.). While researchers and theorists debate the names and stages of each phase of relationship marketing, the concept may be simplified into:

1. An initial interaction.
2. A series of follow-up communications that are assessed in terms of the value added to the customer.

Berry (1995) suggests five strategies to develop relationships: create a core service, customize to the individual, augment with extra services, attract customers via price, and encourage employees to provide good customer service. Ultimately, these strategies result in the customer continuing or terminating his/her relationship with the company, organization, or individual. Social media professionals suggest always adding value to official communications by providing unique or exclusive information unavailable elsewhere in order to solidify customer loyalty and promote continued relationships (Garner et al., 2010).

Relationship marketing inherently requires sport professionals to

- understand the types of communication tools available within both traditional marketing plans as well as in the constantly changing arena of social media.
- know when and how to use the various methods effectively.
- be able to clearly communicate a consistent message to the intended audience.
- effectively assess and revise one's marketing plans.

In addition, keep in mind the unique nature of sports, including their intangible, ephemeral, and subjective aspects, which make events very personal, as well as the perishable nature of sports, which forces people to move on to the next game or event as soon as the current one ends. As a result, it is imperative that sport organizations find creative ways to extend the life of each sporting event and to create meaningful ways for the organization to continue communicating with the consumer.

In addition to the kinds of social media interactions previously mentioned, one of the most crucial methods of building relationships with consumers is through the use of mobile devices. Whether a team sends live updates via text message or offers fans the opportunity to stream games, organizations must provide customers with the ability to stay connected to the team or event even when they cannot attend. Using mobile technology applications such as Banjo, Foursquare, and others (to be covered later in the book) are additional methods to involve fans and drive revenue to your organization or even to your sponsoring organizations. Fans can get discounts by checking into various locations in and around the stadium. Attendees can check in at spots created to highlight events taking place before, during, and after the game. Creative uses of location-based games are great ways to show sponsoring organizations the effectiveness of their sponsorship and generate interest in products and services. At the same time, the interactive nature of the technology combined with the online incentives encourages repeat business and loyalty to the participating organizations.

Two theories that are helpful in understanding how to build relationships with customers via social media are social penetration theory and engagement theory.

Social penetration theory

As individuals share and contribute to the social media landscape they inevitably interact with other individuals and develop online relation-

European sport organizations' use of mobile devices

European sport organizations got a jump on U.S. organizations when it came to using mobile devices. For example, the NBA is a global brand but the New York Knicks are not. However, in Europe, Manchester United is a global brand. As a result, perhaps out of necessity, organizations such as Manchester United have learned to communicate better with the various demographics within their fan base. In fact, their texts are often bilingual; their efforts are global in nature in order to reach fans across the world; and they are adept in modifying their messages to fit the cultural attitudes and beliefs of fans. For example, Manchester United actually reaches out to fans in Bangladesh, Beijing, Singapore, etc., using text messaging and other mediums whereas teams in the United States are much more narrowly focused in sending out team messages en masse (Favorito, 2011).

Some sport organizations in Europe and in the United States use smartphones to increase concession sales. The average time a person spends conducting a transaction at the concession stand is at least 49 seconds, in addition to time spent waiting in line. Once at the counter, a person places an order, is rung up on the register, pays for the items, obtains a receipt (and change if necessary), takes the purchased items and leaves, all in 49 seconds. The transaction of a fan who places an order using a smartphone while watching the game and going up to the concession stand, scanning the phone, hearing a beep indicating payment was made, and taking the items may take as few as 15 seconds. This could translate into a three-fold increase of concession stand sales and provide a more pleasant overall game experience for the fan. It also enables the organization to keep track of who made a purchase, what time it was made, how much the individual spent, what the person bought, etc.—all invaluable information that can be used in a comprehensive marketing plan for the future (Steinbrecher, 2011).

ships. Social penetration theory focuses on the various stages people experience when sharing with others and provides a framework for how relationships develop: orientation of interaction, exploratory affective exchange, affective exchange, and stable exchange stages.

Orientation of interaction. According to Smith's interpretation of Altman and Taylor's work on social penetration (n.d.), this first stage consists of people sharing in small parts. At this point, relationships tend to be somewhat superficial in nature. When a customer begins interacting with a website, it is not uncommon for him/her to simply browse the site, read the posts, and examine the information in a detached manner.

Exploratory affective exchange. This second stage is when people begin to let down their guard and share more personal information as they get to know one another. At this point, a consumer may decide to provide his/her contact information, create a profile, and post basic comments in chat rooms or forums.

Affective exchange. This is a transition period that reflects individuals deciding which relationships are important and warrant continued development. Once a person begins exploring the social media arena he/she often evaluates a variety of sources and participates in many discussion groups. Over time, people tend to scale back their participation to the few sites about which they feel most passionate or with which they have created the strongest bonds.

Stable exchange. This final stage is the highest level in social penetration theory; it is where intimacy is achieved and relationships strengthen. This often culminates in people becoming regular contributors to blogs, or even creating their own sites and linking back to the organization via the detailed persona they have now established (Smith, n.d.). This concept reinforces the ideas mentioned in relationship to the Chicago Fire and FIPPEX software in the box on p. 32. "It is all about the number of touches an organization has with clients and the relationships that are built with key clients and customers" (Steinbrecher, 2011).

Sport organizations must be cognizant of the four stages people progress through as they participate in social media forums. Just as face-to-face relationships take time to develop and grow, so do online interactions. According to representatives of Sports Media Challenge, a company that provides media and communication training, one of the pitfalls of social media occurs when people forget they must be patient, be consistent, and communicate over time in order to build a community, amass a significant following, and earn the trust of those in their online community. This means if you have an event to promote, be sure to promote it early, build up momentum, talk about it consistently online before the event, during the event, and after the event (Garner et al., 2010). Organizations that are customer friendly and offer online help or the ability to communicate with a live person will be able to create, maintain, and benefit from long-term customers. Taking time to plan and develop a site and cultivate relationships is part of the successful social media campaign. It is imperative to know your goals, be realistic in your expectations, and "under sell and over deliver" (Favorito, 2011). One of the benefits of encouraging open communication between customers and the organization is the level of feedback it creates. The two-way communication provides sport organizations with many opportunities to improve on services and experiences, which yields brand loyalty and even increased sales.

Engagement theory

Customer engagement is essential to building relationships and is based upon the repeated interactions between the organization and the customer. Each time the customer is engaged, the emotional, psychological, or physical investment is strengthened between the consumer and the brand (Chaffey, 2007). Consistent with engagement theory, a successful social media campaign entices customers to interact repeatedly. Consultant Joe Favorito advises, however, that social media campaigns should engage the correct people in the process; "I'd rather have the right 2,000 people targeted than the wrong 200,000 people" (Favorito, 2011). Statistics and data should be collected to help evaluate and assess a social media campaign. Data may be collected and analyzed through a variety of web-based tools, which are discussed further in Chapter 9. It is important to note that such measurements include the number of times a person visits a site, the length of time spent on a web page, the number of logins made, and the pathways selected to view web pages.

As your social media campaign grows over time, professionals warn of becoming too overwhelmed with the enormity of an all-encompassing project. To combat this pitfall, periodically reevaluate each platform, method, or vehicle used in the campaign to assess whether or not it is meeting the overall goals and engaging customers. If a channel is not generating the expected results, consider dropping it and focusing on another venue that is working. There is no need to use every social media tool just for the sake of using it; be strategic in managing your resources.

Persuasion Marketing

Persuasion refers to the process by which people use messages to influence others, to change their mindsets, or get people to act (McGaan, 2010). Simply stated, persuasion marketing is designed to get people to take action. Whether the marketer wants to sell tickets to a game or obtain a sponsorship agreement, the ultimate goal is to trigger a person to act in a manner consistent with the marketer's plan. According to McGaan (2010), the foundation of persuasion marketing is the Rational Model of Persuasion. This theory asserts that a person's beliefs (what he/she believes is true or false) added to the individual's values (what he/she thinks is good or bad) and motives (the person's self-interests) will result in specific attitudes (a person's like or dislike), which translate into relatively predictable behaviors (the person's action). To clarify, think of it as a mathematical formula like this:

Beliefs + Values/Motives = Attitudes → Behavior

The key to effectively persuading an individual is to understand the beliefs and values that form the person's attitude toward the given subject. Before a social media campaign can effectively be planned, the organization must have information about the audience and about the organization and its products or services. This is an area that needs improvement in the sport industry, given that few organizations are currently asking their fans enough questions to understand their beliefs and values and to determine their attitudes, which form their behaviors (Favorito, 2011).

Once the sport organization has this information, a marketing professional can then attempt to mold a person's beliefs, values, or attitudes in a particular direction in order to get the person to act favorably toward a specific campaign. In fact, by providing information through a variety of channels to targeted individuals, marketers hope to entice consumers to spend their time, money, and resources within their organization. Persuasion marketing is not necessarily a quick process. In fact, in order to be successful, a marketing campaign must be presented strategically, with repeated exposure to the intended audiences until the message becomes understood, recognized, and accepted. Only then will most people be willing to take action consistent with the marketing campaign's expectations (Hill, n.d.; Virzi, 2011).

An example of utilizing the persuasion theory in sport marketing was the "Basketball Never Stops" ad campaign by Nike. According to Nike, the campaign included a social media campaign with a dedicated Facebook page and Twitter hashtag encouraging fans to "join together to keep the spirit of the game alive throughout the lockout." Nike used persuasion marketing to promote basketball across a variety of age groups with the goal of focusing attention on the sport in general and Nike products in particular. As is generally the case, the persuasion theory technique attempts to influence consumer behavior and result in sales for the company. Sport organizations and professionals must remember that successful social media campaigns take time to create, plan, and implement. Research must be conducted to clearly identify the target audience and to understand their pervasive beliefs, values, motives, and attitudes. Messages must be crafted and delivered repeatedly to reach individuals and gain acceptance before the desired actions and outcomes can be achieved.

CONCLUSION

In order to understand the unique aspects of the sport product and the sport industry, sport marketers must spend time learning about the consumers of sport. Our electronic society enables sport marketers to tap into a variety of sources using social media tools. Organizations can create Facebook pages, Twitter accounts, consumer polls, and many other tools to engage with consumers regarding their products and services. The two-way nature of social media gives the sport marketing professional a variety of avenues to remain in constant contact with the consumers and therefore, promptly respond to all concerns. As a result, sport professionals can and should provide excellent customer service all of the time to sport industry participants.

It is incumbent upon sport professionals to recognize the ways in which social media impacts sport communication and marketing. Efforts to communicate, collaborate, educate, and entertain should be included as part of the sport marketing campaign for individual athletes, sports teams, sports leagues, sport organizations, and educational institutions at all levels. Furthermore, marketing plans must stay current through constant evaluation and updating of the sport organization's or individual's online presence. Feedback from consumers must be taken into account and addressed quickly and appropriately. Moving from the old concept of the 4P's in marketing to the newer 4C's version (outlined earlier in this chapter) will enable sport marketers a basic framework from which to operate.

REVIEW QUESTIONS

1. What makes the sport industry and their products unique?
2. How does social media impact sport marketing?
3. What communication strategies should be used by sport marketing professionals to optimize social media tools?

4. What are the four stages of the social penetration theory? Think of a website or sport team where you believe you have reached the final stage. Explain how you moved through the four stages to get there.

5. Provide two recent examples of specific instances where you think social media tools were successfully used in the marketing plan of a sport product or service.

REFERENCES

Berry, L. L. (1983). Relationship marketing. In L.L. Berry, G. L. Shostack, & G. D. Upah (Eds.), *Emerging perspectives on services marketing* (pp. 25–28). Chicago, IL: American Marketing Association.

Berry, L. L. (1995). Relationship marketing of services—growing interest, emerging perspectives. *Journal of the Academy of Marketing Services, 23*(4), 236–245.

Chaffey, D. (2007). Online customer engagement presentation 2007. Retrieved from http://www.davechaffey.com/presentations-old/customer-engagement-presentation.

Favorito, J. (2011, June 6). Personal communication.

Federal Communications Commission. (2005, November 21). Wired, zapped, and beamed, 1960's through 1980's. Retrieved from http://transition.fcc.gov/omd/history/tv/1960-1989.html.

Garner, D., Patrick, D., Barrett, L., & Lane, B. (2010, July 7). Personal communication.

Hill, P. D. (n.d.). The six stages of persuasion. Retrieved from http://evancarmichael.com/Public-Relations/224/The-Six-Stages-of-Persuasion.html.

Kahle, L. R., & Close, A. G. (Eds.). (2011). *Consumer behavior knowledge for effective sports and event marketing*. New York: Routledge.

Lauterborn, R. (1990). New marketing litany: Four p's passe; c-words take over. *Advertising Age, 26*. Retrieved from http://rlauterborn.com/pubs/pdfs/4_Cs.pdf.

McCombs, M. E., & Shaw, D. L. (1972). The agenda-setting function of mass media. *Public Opinion Quarterly, 36*(2), 176–187.

McGaan, L. (2010, February 11). Introduction to persuasion. Retrieved from http://department.monm.edu/cata/saved_files/Handouts/PERS.FSC.html.

Mullin, J. B., Hardy, S., & Sutton, W. A. (2007). *Sport marketing* (3rd ed). Champaign, IL: Human Kinetics.

Novo, J. (n.d.). Relationship marketing. Retrieved from http://www.jimnovo.com/Relationship-Marketing-more.htm.

Schultz, B., Caskey, P. H., & Esherick, C. (2010). *Media relations in sport* (3rd ed.). Morgantown, WV: Fitness Information Technology.

Smith, R. (n.d.). Altman & Taylor's social penetration theory: Important people in our lives. Retrieved from http://www.pearsoncustom.com/link/humanities/comm/allcomm/socialpenetrationtheory.html.

Social network ad spending to approach $1.7 billion this year. (2010, August 16). Retrieved from http://www.emarketer.com/Article.aspx?R=1007869.

Solis, B., and Thomas, J. (2013). The conversation prism. [graphic] Retrieved from http://www.theconversationprism.com.

Solis, B. (n.d.). The roles of the social consumer. [graphic] Retrieved from http://www.flickr.com/photos/briansolis/5303340481.

Sowell, M. (2008). The birth of national sports coverage: An examination of the New York Herald's use of the telegraph to report America's first "championship" boxing match in 1849. *Journal of Sports Media, 3*(1), 51–75.

Steinbrecher, H. (2011, June 7). Personal communication.

Tuchman, R. (2009). *The 100 sporting events you must see live: An insider's guide to creating the sports experience of a lifetime.* Dallas: Benbella Books.

Virzi, A. M. (2011, August 3). Persuasion marketing tips from Susan Bratton. Retrieved from http://www.clickz.com/click/column/2098794/persuasion-marketing-tips-susan-bratton.

Wampler, G., Johnston, B., Heasley, B., & Newman, T. J. (2011). "Diadora America: A social media case study." Paper presented at 2011 Hawaii International Conference on Education. Honolulu. 4 January, 2011.

Social Networks and Real-Time Platforms

INTRODUCTION

Thus far we've talked a lot about social media and its ever-evolving status. At the core of social media are social networks like Facebook, Twitter, YouTube, and other websites/communication platforms that connect us to the world. While social media is more than just a series of websites, it would indeed be virtually impossible to network with others without these and other aforementioned sites. In this chapter we identify social networking platforms and examine marketing strategies that allow for maximum brand exposure in the sport industry.

You'll notice that we call sites like Facebook, Twitter, and YouTube "social networking platforms" rather than merely social media websites. There is an important distinction between these two terms. The terms *social media* and *social networking* describe different ways of interacting online. We talked a little bit about the definition of social media in Chapter 1 but let's look at it further. Boyd and Ellison (2007) define social networking as "web-based services that allow individuals to construct a public or semi-public profile within a bounded system, articulate a list of other users with whom they share a connection and view and traverse their list of connections and those made by others within the system."

Notice that this definition of social networking does not include the term *website*. Indeed, what started out as websites like Facebook and YouTube has grown to become communication hubs that exist beyond your personal computer screen. Now that we've defined social networking, let us also define the term *social media*.

Kaplan and Haenlein (2010) define social media as "a group of Internet-based applications that build on the ideological and technological foundations of Web 2.0, and that allow the creation or exchange of User Generated Content." The key phrase here is *user generated content,* because that is what drives sites like Facebook, YouTube, and Twitter.

Now that we have defined the difference between social networking and social media, here is a brief overview of how the major social networks are viewed from a marketer's perspective.

MAJOR SOCIAL NETWORKS

 et's take a few minutes to review how Facebook, Twitter, and Google+ grew from humble beginnings into major social websites.

Facebook

Facebook has evolved from a site that emphasizes personal connections to one that focuses on connecting with people, brands, and places of interest. Of particular interest to marketers is the Pages feature, launched in 2007. Facebook pages are profiles designed to allow companies to maintain an official presence on Facebook. Facebook launched custom URLs (also known as "vanity URLs") in 2010, thereby making it much easier for companies to promote their Facebook pages in advertisements.

Facebook's "pages"

In early 2011, Facebook dramatically changed its pages available to businesses. Whereas public profiles for individuals have been around since Facebook's inception, the pages on which businesses can build their own virtual profiles are a more recent development. And Facebook never stands still. In early 2011, the world's largest social network took a much needed step toward improving how brands can market themselves on the site with its revamped pages initiative.

When looking at best practices in regard to their Facebook page, the first question businesses should ask is "what do we want it to do?" These businesses already have websites, and while a Facebook page is arguably more accessible than a website, the fact remains that the website is the old guard while Facebook is the new guard.

It is imperative for businesses to recognize that a Facebook page is something altogether different from its company website. Facebook pages should be more loose, fun, and engaging than the official website. Exhibit 3.1 shows the web home page and Facebook page for the Scottsdale, Arizona, Parks and Recreation department, for example.

EXHIBIT 3.1   Home page and Facebook page for the Scottsdale Parks and Recreation Department.

(continued)

EXHIBIT 3.1   Home page and Facebook page for the Scottsdale Parks and Recreation Department, *continued.*

What should a Facebook page do for your company? It should act as a portal to your website and everything else you do both online and offline. Think of Facebook as a billboard on a frequently traveled highway on the way out of town: People see it because it's right there, where they are. The old adage in real estate—location, location, location—is also the reason why your business needs a strong Facebook presence: Your potential customers are already there.

Features of successful Facebook pages

On Facebook, engagement is about three key ideas:

1. Generating buzz about your brand.
2. Giving your audience something of value.
3. Knowing how to integrate your Facebook page with the other parts of your social media presence.

A successful Facebook page generates buzz for its brand. This means that when visitors land on your Facebook page, they can easily learn more about your brand. If you're a sport team or athlete, that could include upcoming promotions and special Facebook-only sales as well as the very latest on a new signing. Teams drive traffic to their Facebook pages by offering their fans something of value, in many cases discounted tickets or merchandise and sales only available to Facebook fans. For smaller businesses, getting traffic to your Facebook page can seem difficult, but the same incentives apply: Visitors want access to breaking news, behind the scenes photos and videos and exclusive deals. If you give your audience value and put a personal touch on your Facebook page, your audience will slowly grow.

Facebook is an important part of a social plan, but keep in mind that it should complement other strategic elements and not simply overpower them. For example, a social media campaign to publicize a restaurant at your stadium or arena could be centered around directing fans to your Facebook page. By visiting this page, fans will see a custom landing tab that publicizes the new restaurant with information on the menu and the grand opening. Once the restaurant opens, it is important to keep answering questions via Facebook, but it is also important to monitor customer feedback through Twitter, Foursquare, Yelp, and other channels. Essentially, even though Facebook is vital to any social campaign, an organization must also juggle all the other elements of social media at the same time.

Creating an effective page

Keep in mind five key points when creating and maintaining a Facebook page:

1. **Conversation and engagement:** Facebook is a two-way street.
2. **Sell your product:** Promote what you're selling on your website (if applicable).

3. **Call to action:** This gets visitors to move from being passive observers to becoming participants. It can be as simple as encouraging visitors to "like" your brand or a status, or asking them to post or tweet a link to your Facebook page as part of a contest. The most important thing to remember on Facebook (as in traditional web design) is to give your visitors something to do. This keeps them entertained and, most importantly, keeps them on your Facebook page, where you control the message.

4. **Multimedia:** Text is boring. Facebook is the world's largest photo-sharing website for a reason.

5. **Visual impact:** Make it stand out.

In summary, create an eye-catching design that draws attention to your brand, and then provide information on your product along with a call to action.

Communicating effectively on the page

The most successful brands on Facebook owe much of their success to the ongoing dialogue they maintain with fans. Here are a few examples of good questions a sport organization might ask on Facebook:

- What is your favorite promotion at our events?
- What is your favorite memory from last season?
- What's one thing you'd like to see us do differently next season?
- What can we do to improve your experience at (our venue)?

Notice one common element: All of these questions require complete answers. None of them are yes or no questions. An organization can learn much about itself by soliciting the opinions of its Facebook supporters.

While asking questions and responding to fan inquiries is an important component of a successful Facebook page, it goes hand in hand with another of the five features listed above: multimedia.

Look at Exhibit 3.2, taken from the New Jersey Devils' Facebook page in January, 2013.

The Devils are one of the most social media friendly organizations in the NHL. The Devils routinely post photos immediately following games, and the NHL franchise remains active on Facebook even during the offseason. Often on the Facebook page, the organization shares photos of fans wearing Devils gear, plays trivia games through photos,

EXHIBIT 3.2   New Jersey Devils' Facebook page.

Source: www.facebook.com/NewJerseyDevils. Used with permission.

and updates fans on the latest roster moves. The organization's willingness to engage its fans ensures that fans spend time talking about the team on the team's Facebook page.

One of the best elements of a Facebook page is its communal aspect. Your fans are there, discussing your brand, all the time. An organization like the Devils may post a gallery of photos but then move on to other business, such as sending out post-game materials to the traditional media. In the interim, fans are drawn to the gallery—and the Devils brand—on their own time. This is why multimedia is a must on Facebook: It means clicks and eyeballs, and that means exposure.

Facebook pages in action: Two case studies

Let's look at two examples of the call-to-action step on sport-related Facebook pages.

CASE 1: SPORTS AUTHORITY, https://www.facebook.com/SportsAuthority

Despite being a smaller national sporting goods chain, Sports Authority made headlines with its use of social media in 2010 and 2011. The chain was one of the first nationally to embrace the check-in service Foursquare, offering those who became the "mayors" of each of its stores a gift certificate.

Some of the most interesting content that Sports Authority includes on its Facebook page is about its charitable causes, namely Girls on the Run, a national nonprofit that teaches girls the value of fitness and a healthy lifestyle. During the summer and fall of 2011 Sports Authority donated $5.00 to the charity for every "like" it received on its Facebook page. This is a great example of a win-win situation through social media: Sports Authority increases its fan base on Facebook (and its potential marketing reach as well) while Girls on the Run earns donations for each person who "likes" the Sports Authority page.

CASE 2: NIKE BASKETBALL, https://www.facebook.com/nikebasketball

Long considered the most visible individual Nike brand, the Nike Basketball Facebook page acts as a hub for basketball-related fan chatter on Facebook and Twitter and encourages fans to participate in contests and other activities.

Perhaps the most interesting aspect to the Nike Basketball Facebook page is how it testifies to the global appeal of basketball, especially when viewed against the backdrop of the Fall 2011 NBA lockout. Nike Basketball created the #Basketball NeverStops campaign, which encouraged Facebook, Twitter, and Instagram users to share tweets and photos that explain why "basketball never stops." Not only were participants offered a chance to have their tweets posted to the highly trafficked Nike Basketball Facebook page, but they were also entered into a contest to meet NBA stars and Nike brand ambassadors like LeBron James and Kevin Durant.

In both of these examples, we can see that brands are using Facebook as a focal point to energize the vibrant fan community around their brands. Nike Basketball was able to turn a negative situation (the NBA lockout) into a positive one through social media.

In the Sports Authority example, the company used its Facebook page to spearhead a social campaign to help a national charity. In doing so, they demonstrated social responsibility and raised their social media profile at the same time. That's a win-win situation for any brand.

One of the easiest ways for a brand to establish traction on Facebook is to post multimedia materials and encourage others to share theirs. While status updates can be interesting, the true stars of a brand's Facebook page are often its photos and videos, especially those that ask visitors to create a caption or participate in some way.

Brands can take multimedia sharing to the next level, too. Besides simply posting photos and videos on their Facebook page, smart brands understand that multimedia can be a call to action (there's that term again) for its users. For example, brands will often introduce a contest on their Facebook page and ask users to create and upload video responses on YouTube and then tweet links to their videos complete with a brand-created hashtag (i.e., subject keywords added to a tweet, which will be discussed in more detail later). This increases brand visibility virally, through both the videos and the tweets.

The final ingredient of a successful Facebook page is that the page itself should stand out and be memorable. There are millions of Facebook users with personal pages. Brands now understand that their pages should be completely different from personal pages. Remember: Facebook is a social network; it's supposed to be fun. Make your Facebook page a destination for your users.

One final point. While the feel and goals of your organization's website and Facebook page should be different, the Facebook page still should serve as a portal to your organization's online presence. As such, the Facebook application programming interface (API) allows external websites to incorporate Facebook functionality on their own sites. You've probably seen the "sign in with Facebook" prompt across most popular news sites, especially those that offer content sharing tools. The ability to share content on Facebook from anywhere on the Internet—as the share tool enables users to do—is one of the biggest reasons why Facebook is such a titan in the social world. The share tool allows Facebook to reach beyond its Facebook.com domain. It is for this reason that your brand's website should not only link to and feature content from your Facebook page, but also emphasize the share tool to expand content across social platforms.

Simply put, you want to make it as easy as possible for your audience to share your content, whether they're on your Facebook page or not. The Facebook share tools are important to any organization because they do this effectively and easily. Why create an account on yet another website when you can simply login with your Facebook account and share content that way? For the millions of people who have a Facebook account, sharing content through the application is extremely easy—and with the share tools you need not be on Facebook.com to do so.

Twitter

Twitter is the largest real-time social platform in the world. What about Facebook, you ask? While it's true that Facebook is the largest social website in the world, it lacks the inherently open, nearly instantaneous nature that Twitter offers to all users. The key element to Twitter is its timeliness. On Twitter, things can change in a matter of minutes. Prior to founding Twitter, Jack Dorsey worked at Odeo, a small podcasting company in San Francisco. One day, Dorsey had an idea for a service that would allow users to share short messages with groups of people at the same time, something akin to a text message that goes out to groups rather than one individual. Dorsey called the proposed service "twttr" and developed it a short time later. Dorsey wrote the first ever tweet—"just setting up my twttr"—on March 21, 2006. He renamed the service "Twitter" and launched the company in April 2007.

Software engineer Dom Sagolla, who also worked at Odeo, helped launch Twitter with Dorsey. Sagolla (2009), recalling the early days of Twitter, pointed to two key events that helped Twitter grow in its early days: the 2007 South by Southwest (SXSW) festival in Austin, Texas, and the MTV Video Music Awards in September of that same year. Audiences at both events were encouraged to interact with each other via Twitter. Sagolla explained that the exposure from these events served as the application's tipping point.

During Twitter's early days, few businesses maintained accounts on the site. Indeed, Twitter was mostly filled with people looking to connect with friends or anyone with shared interests. As Twitter grew, businesses began establishing official Twitter accounts. Today, there are thousands of businesses on Twitter ranging from small "mom and pop" local businesses to huge multinational corporations. Most sport organizations didn't join Twitter until 2009, a full two years after Twitter experienced its first large-scale wave of growth.

To illustrate the sport industry's slow adoption of Twitter, consider the following list of when popular sport accounts launched on Twitter:

- Shaquille O'Neal, @The_Real_Shaq, November 2008
- Major League Baseball, @MLB, December 2008
- National Football League, @NFL, January 2009

- National Baseball Association, @NBA, February 2009
- National Hockey League, @NHL, June 2009

And here are the join dates of several popular non-sport accounts:

- CNN Breaking News, @CNNbrk, January 2007
- New York Times, @NYTimes, March 2007
- Wall Street Journal, @WSJ, April 2007
- Southwest Airlines, @SouthwestAir, June 2007
- Oprah Winfrey, @Oprah, January 2009

You can see that many bigger brands, especially in the media, joined Twitter in 2007. The sport industry mostly joined Twitter in 2009, although Shaq and Major League Baseball were the industry's early adopters. Now a Twitter account is a necessary and powerful tool in an organization's social media kit.

Creating an effective Twitter profile

Let's review the key elements of a successful Twitter page and discuss how each element can help an organization from a branding standpoint:

1. Username
2. Profile picture
3. Bio paragraph
4. Link
5. Purpose

Username.   Arguably the most important element to any Twitter account is its username. After all, what good is your Twitter account if no one can find you? Your organization's username should be easily recognizable to anyone searching for it on Twitter. For a professional sport team, your username should be either your full name, e.g., the @MiamiDolphins or, simply @Dolphins. For a business or a nonprofit organization, it should be the full name of your organization or a commonly used acronym.

Profile picture.   One often overlooked aspect of a Twitter account is the profile picture. Almost all professional teams use their logo (or some variation) as their profile picture. If you are a social media coordinator, however, it is important to use your own picture on your profile, because you are literally the face and contact person for your organization.

Bio paragraph.   Describe your organization in one sentence. Be clear yet concise. Perhaps tell visitors a bit about how you use your Twitter account or link to more information (see below). If appropriate, share a bit about yourself as social media coordinator. Let people know who's behind the account.

Link.   As a social media coordinator (or simply the person primarily responsible for your organization's Twitter presence), you should mention your association with the organization in your Twitter bio. Alternatively, your organization should mention the name and Twitter handle of the person in charge of your Twitter account, because this gives followers an easy way to get in touch with your organization. Including a link back to your website (or a special social media sub-site) is vital, too.

Purpose: Twitter as a marketing and PR tool

An important aspect of your Twitter presence is its value as a means of being proactive from a public relations (PR) standpoint. While your primary purpose in joining Twitter may have been to engage your audience, being an engaged Twitter participant simply cannot be overlooked. As social media strategist Lisa Buyer told an audience at the PR Conference PubCon 2010 (Harres, 2010), Twitter affords organizations the opportunity to "break up" a press release with quotes and other materials and then "link it back to the full press release on your site." This "breadcrumbs" approach helps journalists and your general audience find more information about your brand and reflects the "social media as a portal" theory discussed earlier.

Google+

Google+ launched into the crowded social media space in the summer of 2011. Despite previous efforts in social networking, Google+ is the largest effort to date from the Internet titan.

At its core, Google+ is similar to Facebook and Twitter. Users are encouraged to share posts and content with others. The primary difference between Google+ and Facebook and Twitter is that Google+

essentially incorporates the sharing element of Facebook and Twitter and the public availability of Twitter into one site. In a sense, Google+ is what Facebook might be if Facebook were more "open" (i.e., users shared content with the general public and not simply their friends).

While users add friends on Facebook and followers on Twitter, they add people to various "circles" on Google+, with an unlimited number of circles that correspond to personal or professional contacts, among others. The practice of adding people to various circles gives the user more control over who sees what content, which is similar to the privacy controls Facebook instituted in 2010 and early 2011.

Although Google+ is still growing, as of 2012 the site had yet to achieve any kind of critical mass beyond the techie crowd. It remains to be seen what impact, if any, Google+ will have on social networking.

LinkedIn and sport marketing careers

While Facebook is the world's largest social networking site, LinkedIn is arguably the world's largest professional networking site. Launched in May 2003, LinkedIn is a sort of Facebook for professional contacts. While the emphasis at Facebook is on personal relationships, the emphasis at LinkedIn is on professional ones—former colleagues, co-workers, interns, employers, and the like. LinkedIn isn't specific to the sport industry but it holds many important lessons for aspiring sport marketers.

First, all current college students should have an up-to-date LinkedIn profile complete with a work history, including internships and recommendations from former colleagues. A complete LinkedIn profile includes current work information, contact information, and an overview of your practical skills and qualifications.

The old adage for the job seeker is that "it's not who you know, it's who knows you." That's the point of LinkedIn: By maintaining an updated profile and connecting with the people you've worked with, you have an "in" at other companies, and having an "in" or a connection can often make the difference between being noticed and being just another resume in a pile.

Although it doesn't get the massive word-of-mouth of Facebook, Twitter, and YouTube, LinkedIn remains a valuable marketing tool for young professionals. The key, as with all social media, is connecting with those around you. Not having a LinkedIn profile is a missed opportunity, especially given how easy it is to simply email your LinkedIn profile to a hiring manager along with a resume. Students and young professionals simply cannot afford *not* to be on LinkedIn.

How fans use social networking

A July 2011 study commissioned by the *Sports Business Journal* found that Facebook is the world's most popular social networking site among sport fans, with Twitter a close second (Broughton, 2011). While it may not be surprising that the world's most popular social networking site is also the most popular with sport fans, it may surprise you to learn how sport fans use Facebook and Twitter—and they do use them differently.

The *Sports Business Journal* survey asked MLB, NFL, NBA, college football, and college basketball fans about their use of social media before, during, and after games. In the first part of the study, these fans were asked about how they use Facebook while watching live sporting events. In all but one instance, fans' use of Facebook increased during their team's game and peaked after the game had ended. The lone exception was NFL fans, whose use of Facebook dropped from 38 percent to 30 percent once the game began. This tells us that fans share in the communal experience of rooting for their favorite teams on Facebook. Fans are watching the game and using Facebook at the same time. For advertisers, this means an extremely captive and engaged audience.

The study also found that fans' use of Twitter also increased during game time and peaked after the game ended, although this differed from sport to sport. Interestingly, professional sport fans used Twitter more as the game went on, while college football and basketball fans' tweeting dropped off once the game began. Still, data supports the overwhelming trend of fans using social media to talk sports with their fellow fans.

Perhaps the single most exciting conclusion from the *Sports Business Journal* survey was what fans identified as the second most popular sport social networking site: YouTube. Why is this? Think about the site's fundamental purpose. It's a search engine for online videos and a gigantic clip archive. When we're talking about sports, we're talking about sports clips, so it makes sense that YouTube would be a popular destination. Yet despite the fact that YouTube features taped video clips (instead of live sports), fans chose YouTube as their second most popular site to talk sports after Facebook. Twitter finished third in the same survey and Facebook Places ranks fourth.

In an interview with the *Sports Business Journal* (Broughton, 2011), NFL spokesman Brian McCarthy said that the study results confirmed the league's own internal research on social media. "More consumption and conversation centered around content leads to fans staying longer on our websites, buying more merchandise and viewing more games," McCarthy stated.

More than simply confirming the NFL's own internal research, the *Sports Business Journal* survey confirms what organizations must know about social media: "The key to success in social media is tapping into the audience's enthusiasm, engaging them, and using that relationship as a call to further action, be it sales, positive public relations, or word-of-mouth marketing."

THE SOCIAL NETWORK MEDIA PLAN

When planning the use of social media, the biggest questions an organization must ask itself are, "What is our message and/or purpose for being here?" and "Who are we trying to reach?" The answers to these questions will help define the company's entire social media strategy.

An organization's Twitter and Facebook pages are perhaps best served as information hubs and portals to everything related to the organization. Many businesses now create custom landing pages for their Facebook pages so that when a user visits their Facebook.com/[business name] website, they see the "mini site" first. The general idea is to inform your audience and motivate them to action, whether that action is to buy tickets to a game or learn more about a new player on the team. In this sense, a properly maintained Facebook page serves as an informal portal to the official website or ticketing website. As with all social media, engagement is key.

In this sense, Facebook is always step one in an online marketing plan. If the goal is to sell tickets, for example, you can reach fans through Facebook or Twitter (or a different site), but then you need to coax them to visit your official website (or the ticket website) to actually buy tickets. Because nearly all fans are familiar with Facebook, it is easier to direct them to your organization's Facebook page than it is to ask them to go to a ticket sales website where you cannot monitor how long they spend on the site or how they interact with other fans (as you can with Facebook analytics). This is why Facebook and Twitter remain the first step in a social media plan: You use them to funnel customers in and then call them to action (in this example, to buy tickets).

Identifying the Message

An organization must first determine what message it wants to send through social media and how the social media plan will integrate into more traditional print and digital marketing. Once this is done, the organization can move forward in identifying its audience.

Identifying the Audience

How do organizations identify their audience on sites like Facebook and Twitter? How does an organization draw in visitors, apart from its fans, to its social media profiles? As with any traditional marketing plan, a social media marketing plan must contain specific objectives whose results can be measured easily.

For example, if you work for a ticketing company that sells tickets to sporting events, concerts, and theater shows, you have to ask yourself what you want to promote specifically: one type of event, or events during a particularly slow part of the year are two options. Let's say you want to promote the latter, because ticket sales are slow in late winter and early spring, when the weather is uncooperative across most of the country. So, let's say you've determined that you want to promote sporting events, concerts, and plays taking place at a certain venue from January until March. How do you narrow your focus enough to promote shows during this time period without alienating your larger audience?

In this example, our goal is twofold: to promote and sell tickets to these events during a three-month period while also promoting the venue and events taking place year-round (especially since larger concerts typically take place in the summertime). Let's create a content schedule to promote these shows. The shows we want to promote are in January, so we want to begin promoting them in October or November, when tickets are likely to go on sale for the first time. Let's dedicate Tuesdays and Thursdays to promoting these select shows and the rest of the days to promoting our regular schedule.

In order to identify our target audience for these shows, we'll do a few different things. First, we'll scour Twitter and Facebook to find fans of those teams or artists who are playing our venue during our select dates. Then we'll reach out to them with a tweet, inviting them to check out our great deals to see their favorite team/artist at our venue. We'll also cross-promote our deals to fans who have purchased tickets from us in the past. Although this method is typically reserved for email newsletter blasts, we can take the same content and use it in a more immediate way through social media.

One of the best things about social media is how easy it is to identify people based upon interests. Often they will identify themselves as fans of a brand by posting or tweeting about it. This makes it easy to identify fans and, therefore, potential buyers. No matter the goal, a clear marketing plan is integral to social media success. The more specific the plan, the clearer the path is to achieving the objective.

Here is another example. Let's say you work for a team that is planning to advertise its newest partial season ticket packages to its fans via its website. Your boss tells you that employees are encouraged to direct fans to the website for additional information. If the general strategy is to educate fans on these new plans, a team has several ways to accomplish this goal without social media: a direct mailer, phone calls to past customers, and the team's website. How does social media fit into this strategy?

The goal is to educate fans about new ticketing plans, and most of the information is available on the team's website. As discussed earlier, an organization's social media presence acts as an extension of its brand. A fan may find a team's website in seconds with a Google search, or she may not think to visit the site at all. By cross-posting information on sites like Facebook and Twitter, the team increases the scope of its message and thereby reaches a larger audience than it would by relying on the website, print materials, and phone calls alone.

Identifying the Medium

Once your organization identifies its message, it must then determine which medium it wants to emphasize as part of its marketing push. Although Facebook, Twitter, YouTube, and perhaps even Google+ or Ustream are sure to be a part of any social media push, it is important for an organization to prioritize allocating its resources to make the biggest impact from a marketing standpoint. Facebook is likely to be the most important site in any social media plan simply because of its sheer number of users, but, for example, YouTube is incredibly valuable to an organization for sharing video content (content that can also be embedded on a Facebook page). The decision on how to allocate resources is up to the organization but, in most cases, Facebook, Twitter, and YouTube are the most important sites in any campaign. Indeed, while the medium has changed, the basic marketing tenet of tailoring your message to your audience still holds true.

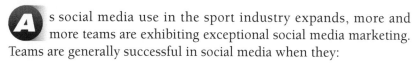

EXAMPLES OF GOOD SOCIAL MEDIA WORK

As social media use in the sport industry expands, more and more teams are exhibiting exceptional social media marketing. Teams are generally successful in social media when they:

- Provide timely updates.
- Engage fans in conversations (Twitter is a two-way street).
- Create a personal identity, giving fans the names and contact information of anyone who regularly updates the organization's Facebook and Twitter pages.
- Connect the social world by organizing such events as meetups to help virtual relationships mature into physical ones (ticket sales, sponsorships, etc.).

- Provide social media promotions that give fans something of value in the form of exclusive social media–only discounts.

While a successful social media strategy is generally complex, it includes simple elements that anyone can implement in less than an hour. A successful social media presence includes timely updates and information on the person or people who represent the company in the social space and their contact information. A photo and links are must-haves, too. A user may have found the company on Twitter and be unaware of its official website. A well-placed link addresses this issue.

In short, a social media page is an extension of your brand. A company needs to be accessible to visitors via social media in the same way it is accessible to those who call the company's office. Let's take a look at some successful social media campaigns and why they work so well.

Teams

Professional sports teams' use of social media varies in the same way that the level of talent on a roster varies—some teams do well while others struggle to keep pace. While there are examples of strong social media work in each league, one key trend has emerged: the smaller the market, the more creative the team's use of social media. Here are a few examples of teams that used social media to grow their brands.

Milwaukee Bucks

The Milwaukee Bucks finished the 2009 NBA season and entered the playoffs as the sixth seed in the Eastern Conference. While the Bucks lost their seven-game, first-round series to Atlanta, the team made headlines for its inventive social media campaign late in the season and during the playoffs. The campaign was entitled "Fear the Deer!"

The Bucks built the "Fear the Deer!" campaign around bloggers, Twitter, and YouTube. At the time the campaign launched, the Bucks had six players regularly using Twitter, including stars Andrew Bogut and Brandon Jennings, and team broadcaster Jim Paschke in addition to the team's official account. The Bucks encouraged bloggers like Bucks fan Jeremy Schmidt, who runs the popular Bucks blog "Bucketball," to spread the campaign to their readers. The team also filmed special "Fear the Deer!" videos and showed them at games and posted them to YouTube. By unifying players, broadcasters, and fans under the same social media campaign, the Bucks generated an energetic discussion about the team's playoff push via social media.

Cleveland Indians

The Milwaukee Bucks aren't the only small-market team making head-lines due to their use of social media. The MLB Cleveland Indians were in the midst of a rebuilding year in 2009 when they made headlines for their own social media efforts. The Indians launched the "Indians Social Media Deck" at Progressive Field during the season. The Deck was a first-of-its-kind space devoted exclusively to social media users. It con-sisted of a raised section of seats in the left field grandstand with HDTV and localized WiFi for patrons. The Indians Social Media Deck was in-vite-only at first, but the Indians have since started taking applications for sports bloggers and others active in social media in greater Cleveland who want to use the deck during a game. More recently, the Indians re-located the social media area from the deck to a dedicated skybox, but its purpose remains to entertain and cater to social media-savvy fans.

St. John's Red Storm

As another example, in 2009 St. John's University in New York City named Peter Robert Casey as its first ever "Twitter beat writer." Casy's job was to cover the St. John's men's basketball program during the 2009–2010 NCAA season. Casey tweeted breaking news, scores, links to interviews, and more during the season. Indeed, his sole job was to provide coverage of St. John's college basketball exclusively through Twitter. While Casey was the first "Twitter beat writer," he will certainly not be the last.

Charlotte Bobcats

In a similar move, the Charlotte Bobcats advertised for the team's first-ever fan blogger in September 2010. The fan blogger joined the Bobcats regular staff in covering the team throughout the 2010–2011 NBA sea-son. Fans were asked to submit a 500-word essay explaining why they would be the best person for the position, and the successful candidate would have their writing featured on the Bobcats website throughout the season. Look for this trend to continue as more and more users mold social media for their own purpose.

Retailers

The national sporting goods chain Sports Authority operates over 450 stores in 45 states across the country. Since being taken private in 2006, Sports Authority has embraced social media and become one of the most social-media friendly sporting good retailers in the country. In January 2011, Sports Authority partnered with ESPN's Winter X Games 15 in Aspen, Colorado, to raise money for breast cancer awareness. Fans were told to check the X Games on Foursquare. Sport Authority donated $1 for each check in (up to $1,000 a day) to Boarding for Breast Cancer, a nonprofit X Games partner.

In March 2011, Sports Authority became an official launch partner for Foursquare 3.0, its updated version of the Foursquare smartphone application. Sports Authority held a contest for shoppers at each of its stores. Each day of the contest, which ran from March 11 through April 9, one store would give away a gift card to any customer who checked in to the store via Foursquare after 11 a.m. (Butcher, 2011).

"Foursquare has a young base, and we have tech adopters, and so it is a pretty nice fit for us," Clay Cowan, vice president of e-commerce and digital marketing at Sports Authority, told the Mobile Commerce Daily weblog. "We're trying to market where our customers are, and our data shows that our web traffic via mobile devices continues to go up, and traffic via Foursquare and Shopkick (a rival geo-location service) continue to skyrocket" (Butcher, 2011, unpaged).

Sports Authority isn't the only retailer making waves with its social media presence. New York City–based sporting goods retailer Modell's, which operates more than 130 stores primarily in the Northeastern United States, uses YouTube to promote its brand with a series of videos that has gone viral. Modell's filmed New England Patriots star Danny Woodhead, Philadelphia Eagles star DeSean Jackson, and New York Knicks star Landry Fields each selling their own jerseys in a local Modell's to unsuspecting patrons. As of this writing, the Woodhead video, the first in the series, had received over 1.6 million views on YouTube. The Jackson and Fields videos had received approximately 350,000 and 670,000 views, respectively.

While we have focused on two brief examples, the takeaway is that retailers understand that they can engage customers and potential customers via social media, both online and in their stores. Retailers are willing to try new things to reach new customers and embracing social media allows them to do just that.

The Fans

Fans are by far the largest segment of the social media population—they *are* the audience. Businesses must recognize and cater to their audience, and sport organizations are no different. "We want people talking about the team," Kyle Rogers (2010), digital strategist for the Sporting Kansas City MLS soccer team, says. Rogers says that teams must recognize the difference between the chatter about a team's on-field performance and the chatter about its business operations.

"In general, chatter about on-field play is always a good thing," Rogers says. "Now if they have had a bad experience around something that is controlled or facilitated by the staff off the field, that's a time to jump in and try to help." Rogers's statement reflects a simple truth about social media: A large part of a company's social media presence involves monitoring what's being said about their brand on blogs and Twitter. A proactive team is a prepared team.

The Athletes

Professional athletes use Twitter to talk directly to both their fans and their critics. Indeed, the days of an athlete relying on the traditional media to tell his or her side of the story are long gone. An athlete nowadays needs only to tweet, write a blog post, or record a video to YouTube or Ustream to reach fans. These missives are often entertaining glimpses into the lives of professional athletes.

While social media can be a useful tool to professional athletes, this unfiltered medium can create problems, too. Sites like Facebook and Twitter give athletes a means to address fans directly. While this direct link to the audience is usually a good thing, it can also land an athlete in hot water. Indeed, since professional athletes took Twitter by storm in 2009, a plethora of athletes have learned firsthand the potential downside of using social media.

In June 2009, Minnesota Timberwolves forward Kevin Love let slip that then-head coach Kevin McHale would not return to coach the team the following season. Love tweeted, "Today is a sad day. . . Kevin McHale will NOT be back as head coach this season." While McHale knew he was being let go at the time, the information was not public knowledge until Love's tweet. Love later apologized for the gaffe.

Love's tweet was a simple mistake. For better or worse, athletes are in the spotlight all the time, even on Facebook and Twitter. In fact, many pro teams now classify social media under the same general guidelines as traditional media. This means that players must watch what they write at all times. It only takes one ill-advised tweet to stir up unnecessary controversy.

Some athletes have even been fined for their tweets. The NFL was one of the first leagues to ban its players from tweeting during games.

The NFL bars players from posting tweets for 90 minutes before and immediately following games. Outspoken wide receiver Chad Johnson, then with the Cincinnati Bengals, tweeted less than 90 minutes before kickoff of a preseason game in August 2010. The NFL fined him $25,000 for violating the league's social media policy.

Here are some common social media "don'ts" for athletes:

- If you wouldn't say it in front of a microphone during media availability, don't say it on Twitter.

- Think before you tweet: If what you post can be interpreted as racist, sexist, or vulgar in any way, you must assume that it will be interpreted this way; therefore, don't post it (perception is reality).

- Remain respectful of your personal and organizational sponsorships (if you are sponsored by Nike, don't tweet a photo of you wearing Adidas gear, for example).

- Mind your associations: Your friends or followers are often public, so understand that the people you associate with reflect on your judgment.

The single most important mantra for athletes using social media is to think before posting/tweeting/commenting, etc. In a world of 24/7 social media, news breaks in a matter of seconds. Athletes may not think the media follows them all the time, but their Facebook and Twitter fans are omnipresent and they monitor their heroes constantly.

CONCLUSION

Since 2009 professional and collegiate teams, leagues, and athletes have used social media to promote their brands. The sport industry uses social media to promote upcoming games and events, sell tickets and sponsorships, and even to advertise new vacancies on the teams and leagues.

Social media is an evolving and versatile medium, but it is not a replacement for traditional marketing and public relations. A company's official Facebook or Twitter page is better used as a complementary element than as a standalone product. Social media should never take the place of a complete company website or traditional, offline marketing materials.

As teams, leagues, athletes, and fans become more comfortable with social media, the industry as a whole will find new ways to utilize it. While the ways professionals use social media to network, interact, and market will change, one thing is certain: Social media is now an important and integral part of any professional business culture.

REVIEW QUESTIONS

1. What is the difference between social networking and social media? Give an example of each term from the chapter text.
2. What are three elements of any successful social networking campaign?
3. Name two of the five key elements of a successful Facebook page.
4. Name three potential negative ramifications of an athlete or organization using social media. Why is it important for an organization to have guidelines for social media use?
5. In what ways does marketing via social media differ from traditional offline marketing? In what ways is it similar?

REFERENCES

Boyd, D. M., & Ellison, N. B. (2007). Social network sites: Definition, history and scholarship. *Journal of Computer-Mediated Communication, 13*(1), article 11. Retrieved from http://jcmc.indiana.edu/vol13/issue1/boyd. ellison.html.

Broughton, D. (2011, June 27). Survey spots social media trends among fans. *Sports Business Daily.* Retrieved from http://www.sportsbusinessdaily.com/ Journal/Issues/2011/06/27/Research-and-Ratings/Social-media.aspx.

Butcher, D. (2011, March 11). Sports Authority distributes mobile deals via Foursquare to drive foot traffic. *Mobile Commerce Daily.* Retrieved from http:// www.mobilecommercedaily.com/2011/03/11/sports-authority-distributes- mobile-deals-via-foursquare-to-drive-foot-traffic.

Harres, V. (2010, Nov. 15). Twitter, social media and PR: Stats and tactics. http://blog.prnewswire.com/2010/11/15/twitter-social-media-and-pr-stats- tactics/.

Kaplan, A. M., & Haenlein, M. (2010, Jan.–Feb.). Users of the world, unite! The challenges and opportunities of Social Media. *Business Horizons, 53*(1): 59–68. Retrieved from http://www.sciencedirect.com/science/article/pii/ S0007681309001232.

Rogers, K. (2010). Personal interview conducted by Brendan Wilhide.

Sagolla, D. (2009). How Twitter was born. Retrieved from http://www.140 characters.com/2009/01/30/how-twitter-was-born/.

Blogging

INTRODUCTION

Prior to the explosion of the Internet, sport organizations depended on traditional media outlets to be their voice. Newspapers, radio, and television stations assigned reporters to cover the hometown team. These reporters attended home games and often traveled to away games, reporting the scores, games, and interesting tidbits about the players. Accurate or not, the reporter's voice represented the team's voice, and the media controlled how the message was delivered.

Advances in broadcasting and technology, specifically the emergence of online and mobile media, have disrupted this model. Today, while traditional media outlets remain an important aspect of the business, organizations cannot afford to wait for these outlets to report their news. Traditional media can be slow in providing coverage (who wants to wait for the 11 p.m. sports roundup on the local TV station?), and news has become tremendously fragmented with technology platforms that can deliver content 24 hours a day.

We discussed in Chapter 1 that, instead of allowing these traditional outlets to control the message, today's sport organizations can link directly to their fans. One of the best methods for directing key messages is a blog. Blogging has become an influential method for an organization to communicate its message to attract viewers to a website or a dedicated blog. A blog gives a voice to anyone in the sport field as well as to passionate fans who have something to say.

In 2010 eMarketer claimed that the number of bloggers had risen 31 percent in just three years. In real numbers this translated into 26.2 million Internet users who updated their blogs at least monthly, and by the end of 2011 the number of active bloggers was projected to reach 28.1 million. Needless to say, this is a critical area any sport marketer needs to capture.

A popular blog can reach a potential audience into the millions. In 2012 eMarketer estimated that nearly 74 million Internet users would read a blog by the end of 2013 (Exhibit 4.1).

WEBSITES AND BLOGS

Look at the top 10 sport websites and the top 10 sport blogs, shown in Exhibit 4.2. What you do not see in these lists are specific websites for professional sports leagues, with the exception of MLB. Someone else is providing the content that the league and teams could be providing for viewers and keeping these fans on their websites and preventing them from clicking on another website.

These sport-related sites have successfully taken the information and reporting on teams and developed good content that people want to read. They also offer fans the opportunity to provide feedback and

EXHIBIT 4.1 United States' blog readers, 2010–2016.

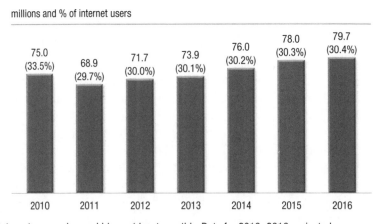

millions and % of internet users

2010	2011	2012	2013	2014	2015	2016
75.0 (33.5%)	68.9 (29.7%)	71.7 (30.0%)	73.9 (30.1%)	76.0 (30.2%)	78.0 (30.3%)	79.7 (30.4%)

Note: Internet users who read blogs at least monthly. Data for 2013–2016 projected.

Source: eMarketer.com, March 2012. Data used with permission.

EXHIBIT 4.2   Most visited sports websites and blogs in the U.S.

TOP 10 SPORTS WEBSITES	TOP 10 MOST POPULAR SPORT-RELATED BLOGS
(based on a June 2011 ranking by Experian Hitwise)	(based on a November 2011 ranking by Technorati.com)
1. Yahoo! Sports	1. bleacherreport.com
2. ESPN	2. mlbtraderumors.com
3. Yahoo! Sports Major League Baseball	3. Dr. Saturday—NCAAF Yahoo! Sports (Rivals.com)
4. Yahoo! Sports NBA	4. *LA Times* Sports Blog
5. Rivals.com	5. Deadspin
6. FOX Sports on MSN	6. ESPN.com NFC West Blog
7. Major League Baseball	7. ESPN.com AFC West Blog
8. ESPN.com-MLB	8. Beyond the Box Score
9. Yahoo! Sports NFL	9. The Hockey Writers
10. Yahoo! Sports NHL	10. ESPN.com AFC North Blog

talk with other fans via the comments sections. Although not yet in the top 10, some sport organizations have realized the benefit in bringing the conversation to their own website. For example, the NFL, through its website, www.NFL.com, has been posting content to its blog since June 2008. It has also broken down blog postings into several categories, including Super Bowl, Pro Bowl, Senior Bowl, the NFL Films Blog, the NFL Network Blog, and Fantasy. These sub-categories deliver targeted content to fans.

Because the league does not play games between February and August, this content is crucial for keeping readers engaged in the sport year-round.

WHY CREATE A BLOG?

People who enjoy sports start blogs for a number of reasons. For passionate fans, it gives them an opportunity to tell a story and to take a position on a subject that matters to them. Using the Internet as their platform, they have the potential to be heard by people around the world.

For a sport organization, initiating one or more blogs on its established website provides an additional outlet to convey information and perspective. The organization has a unique advantage by having an insider's view of the team, sport, players, or product—a point of view that can be interesting to both fans and customers. While teams will certainly not want to give away any trade secrets, the blog might disclose why a general manager or a head of scouting made a certain decision. Popular players can share what they do off the field or in the community, from their own point of view and in their own words.

Blogs that appear within sport websites add depth and perspective to the overall website. In addition, the content created for any blog can potentially bring new fans to the site. How? Consider this: According to Go-Globe.com, in 2011 there were 694,445 Google searches every 60 seconds on the Internet. A portion of those searches involved sports fans looking for information. Blog content is indexed in popular search engines such as Google, Bing, and AOL. Therefore, the more dynamic the content an organization creates around its products, its team, players, or team culture, the easier it will be for people searching the Internet to find the organization's content and its website.

Blogs created for an organization's website will increase the chances of these new viewers clicking over and entering the website portal when they are doing searches. However, if the blog is not linked to a website, a "click for more information" link will probably lead them to the standalone blogging platform. This can be a lost opportunity to capture more views from fans on the organization's website and to generate sales or other desired actions on the site.

BLOGGING PLATFORMS

Some of today's popular blogging platforms include Blogger, WordPress, Tumblr, and Typepad.

While Blogger and Tumblr are free, there is a fee for using Typepad (ranging from $8.95 to $29.95 monthly) and various versions of WordPress are fee-based, depending on the need to customize the look and feel of the site. See the box for a comparison of blogging platforms.

Here are some things to keep in mind when it comes to choosing a platform:

Is a free web-hosted service an option?

If an organization wants a site that hosts all of its files and automatically updates new versions of the software, then it should consider using a free service such as Blogger. With this service there is no need for

Comparison of blogging platforms

WORDPRESS http://wordpress.com

This is one of the most popular blogging platforms on the web, and users can sign up for a free blog at Wordpress.com or download the open source software from Wordpress.org and install on a private web hosting space. WordPress can easily be integrated into a Content Management System to build websites that are more complex than the typical blog.

DRUPAL http://drupal.org

While Drupal may be too advanced for some users, this Content Management System features the flexibility you need to build exactly the kind of website or blog you want. To use Drupal, the software must be downloaded and installed to a private web-hosting space.

BLOGGER http://blogger.com

Owned and operated by Google, Blogger (a.k.a. BlogSpot) is another very popular, free blogging platform. Although very similar in form and function to WordPress, Blogger is more "bare bones" and caters more specifically to blogs and news sites.

TYPEPAD http://typepad.com

TypePad operates using the Movable Type publishing software and is available at three different subscription levels in the United States. The advantages of the TypePad platform include complete design customization, photo albums, and domain mapping.

LIVEJOURNAL http://livejournal.com

Easily the most informal of free blogging platforms, LiveJournal is geared toward young people and those who may be new to blogging.

TUMBLR http://tumblr.com

Tumblr has become known for its emphasis on attractive blog designs, photoblogging, and compatibility with sites such as Twitter, Google Analytics, and Feedburner. While Tumblr is one of the most popular blogging sites, many use it more as a community where blogs are "followed" and posts are "re-blogged" by other users.

Source: Adapted from University of Chicago, "Blogs." Retrieved from http://hub.uchicago.edu/guide/blogs#software. Used with permission.

adding plug-ins or for updating software; everything is self-contained within the main, personalized log-in area. It is the most basic of the free platforms and also the easiest to use for beginners.

However, if an organization is seeking a unique look, customization may be a key factor in the decision process. Some blogging platforms provide templates that make your entries look more professional. If you are integrating it as part of a website, these platforms provide enough flexibility to make the pages look and feel like it is part of the website's overall design. Staff will not need to learn how to code pages, but they will need to learn the basic technology for moving around the back end of a platform's setup.

Visitor statistics are important if your organization wants to make money by adding sponsored elements or online advertisers to its site, and not all platforms support free statistics add-ons. Also, keep in mind free sites like Google Analytics work well with some of the platforms. Many of the blogs provide direct plug-ins (software that can be downloaded into the blog platform to increase and add features) that can help connect Google Analytics to the blog.

Will technical support be needed?

Free, web-based services come with little or no customer support, while paid services offer either phone support or email support to help users solve common problems. If outside assistance will be needed from time to time, this might be a good investment to consider when deciding which direction to go.

Is a free discussion board available to help with technical questions?

Almost all services have a free discussion board where active users help each other.

Is automated spam protection available?

Some sites have filters that read incoming messages or comments on what bloggers post online. This can be configured to read and hold comments before they are posted in a public forum. Why is this important? Some less-than-credible online businesses like to post comments and try to redirect traffic to their shady online sales sites, and protection services can help block these unwanted comments.

CREATING THE BLOG ENTRY

A good blog provides unique content to its readers. This can come in the form of the written word, pictures, and audio and video content. The posted content helps to educate the reader on a subject or a perspective. It can be used to provide insight or a behind-the-scenes look that most fans never get to experience.

Most of all, a good blog will entertain the reader. When we experience interesting, fun, or informative information and enjoy the experience, we are much more likely to remember the blog and bookmark it for a return visit at a later time. Hyperlinks, or highlighted words that provide a link to additional information on a specific subject, add value to any blog post.

Whether you are an experienced writer or someone just starting out as a blogger, you are probably asking yourself, what makes compelling content? What is the magic formula that will keep people coming back for more?

Deciding on Content

Just as with a traditional media outlet, each organization needs to decide what type of online content it should publish.

Let's examine some options a college sports information department might consider as content for its blog. If the university's athletic department wants to educate its readers about the college, it may focus a blog post on the school's mascot. This might include the history of how the mascot came to represent the school. Another blog entry might provide insight into what it takes to be a mascot, describing the time it takes, the physical requirements, and the monetary considerations or other benefits for wearing the funny costume. Finally, another blog entry might include telling a few funny stories about the mascot's most embarrassing moments, biggest surprises, or how he or she made people laugh during a home game.

The history piece might be a 1,000-word essay with an archived photo of school elections. When the athletic department wants to write

Stay updated and find inspiration by reading other blogs

One of the best ways to learn what makes for a successful blog entry is to read them yourself. Reading other people's blogs will give you a sense of what works and what should be avoided.

One popular destination to begin your search is SBNation.com, a website that comprises more than 300 individual sport blogs. With an audience of more than 20 million unique visitors per month, SBNation.com is composed of a network of writers who provide a fresh perspective on sports and specific teams.

about the physical requirements of becoming a mascot, it might provide an interview with the mascot and show photos to illustrate how difficult the process is. Finally, the funny stories may be best shown in an edited video. Keep the video relatively short (three minutes or less) and bring the reader into the video by showing scenes that can make him or her laugh. Once you have determined the type of content you want in your entries, it should be incorporated within regularly scheduled blog posts.

Deciding on Titles for Your Posts

People scan information quickly on the Internet, so your post title needs to grab the reader's attention. You, as a writer, have a very short window to engage the reader with your content. This title is also important for providing an accurate picture for search engines that will index blog posts for readers to find. Does the title of the article relate to the name of the website or its general content in any way? If your site's web address relates to surfing, a blog post with a title "Taking Out the Trash" might not be the most effective way for search engines to index your blog. Try to find something short and catchy. The headline should be a maximum of five words in order to be effective: the shorter, the better. An example might be "Top Five Winter Surfing Destinations."

POSTING YOUR ENTRIES

When it comes time to create a blog entry, either on your organization's site or as a guest on another, you will likely see an area to write and edit your content that looks much like the one shown in Exhibit 4.3. Here you can add the title of your entry and begin writing in the box below. The configuration is set up much like a word processing program.

You can easily bold, italicize, and format your blog text as well as create embedded links within each entry. At the bottom of the box, an automated word count helps track the length of your post.

Blogs entries do not have to be 2,000-word essays. In fact, they should be just the opposite. Blog writing is often more effective when written in short form. Each entry however, does need to meet minimum requirements. When writing, consider as a general rule that each entry should have a minimum of 200 words. It can certainly be longer,

EXHIBIT 4.3 Example of a WordPress blog content editing box.

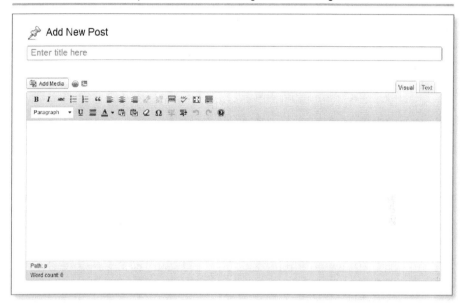

but remember that you must provide enough content to keep your audience interested in the subject matter. Once you are finished with the main portion of your post, consider a few other items. You may want to attach a related photo to the post. The Internet is a visual place, so photos help bring your story to life and are useful in linking your content. More about that a bit later in this chapter.

Also, think about other visual elements such as graphs, charts, and even infographics, like those shown in Exhibit 4.4 (more information on photos and other elements will be discussed in Chapter 5). These colorful graphics help make a point to readers in a visual way that augments the written word.

You should also consider where the blog post might benefit from hyperlinks. Add a hyperlink if you think a word, term, name, or team name might cause readers to want to read more in order to better appreciate your post. However, keep in mind that links can take readers away from your site, and they may not immediately return. Another valuable hyperlink is one that links readers to content *within* your site. For example, if you post a story about attendance numbers for the year, you can link to posts about previous years' attendance (see Exhibit 4.5 for an example from Yahoo! Sports, one of the earliest adopters of intra-linking).

EXHIBIT 4.4   Example of an infographic on a sports blog.

I am not a designer. I admit it. However, I have been fascinated by all of the cool infographics that have been showing up online lately. I have mentioned them and posted a few here in the last two weeks. This includes the Facebook vs Twitter Infographic or the 2011 Obsessed with Facebook Infographic.

This morning, I got up determined to create my first-ever sports infographic. I have not seen many online. The closest I have ever seen something like this in the sports world is the USA Today Snapshots from the printed paper. I stumbled across the salaries page on ESPN.com and thought that would be a good place to start.

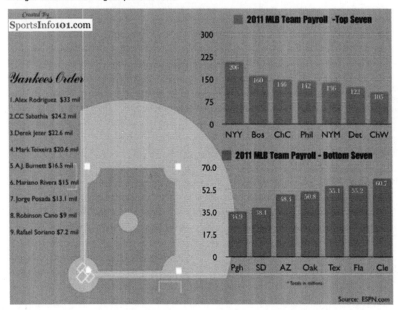

As a former PR man for the Dodgers, I was always taught to stay away from talking abut salaries. It was just not done. In today's terms it is common knowledge. So I set out to create a graphic that showed the top seven teams in terms of 2011 Major League Baseball team salaries as well as the bottom seven teams in total compensation.

With the Largest payroll in Baseball at $206+ million, the Yankees also received special attention in this graphic. On the left, as you can see I have listed the top nine individual salaries for the 2011 Yankee players with Alex Rodriguez leading the list at $33 million dollars.

I learned from this that Rodriguez just about the same salary as the entire Pittsburgh Pirates team. If you, the reader, share this on Facebook, Twitter or other social media, then I'll know the graphic was a hit. Now, you tell me.

This infographic and accompanying blog appeared on Sportsinfo101.com in March 2011 and helped the three-year-old blog register a single-day record number of hits. More than 1,000 people visited in just one 24-hour period. The short title (2011 MLB Team Payroll) is sure to attract the interest of people searching for MLB salary information.

Source: Sportsinfo101.com, http://www.sportsinfo101.com/baseball/2011-mlb-team-salaries-infographic. Used with permission.

EXHIBIT 4.5   Hyperlinks within a Yahoo! Sports post

Jim Mora Jr., UCLA coach, didn't know Cordell Broadus was Snoop Dogg's son when offering a scholarship

   By Cameron Smith | Prep Rally – 2 hours 3 minutes ago

     0

In recent days America has been introduced to Cordell Broadus, the 14-year-old son of rapper Snoop Dogg who suddenly received a football scholarship to UCLA despite spending his first year at Diamond Bar (Calif.) High on the school's freshman team.

This story about a new player at UCLA links back to a previous article ("Snoop Dogg's son Cordell Broadus lands football scholarship offer from UCLA, new home of P-Diddy's son Justin Combs") that first broke the news about Cordell Broadus. This provides context for readers who aren't caught up on the news and also keeps them on the Yahoo! Sports site.

Source: Yahoo! Sports.

Establishing an Internet Voice

When starting a blog, think about developing your Internet voice. What do you want to say and how do you want to say it? When writing on behalf of an organization, keep in mind that everything you say is a direct reflection on your employer. You have a virtual microphone in your hand and everyone can hear you. Here are some fundamental do's and don'ts when it comes to writing for an organization's website.

DO:

- Provide insight in each blog post.
- Be honest and truthful in your writing.
- Create real value for the reader.
- Show a unique perspective from behind the scenes.
- Make them want to return to the site.
- Always remember you are writing for fans or customers.

DON'T:

- Share privileged information unless it has been cleared for publication.
- Make improper comments.
- Use foul language.
- Put down a player, coach, or executive.

When organizing the content of a blog, think like a writer. Develop and express key messages in every post. Let's create a hypothetical blog post using some of the Do's and Don'ts mentioned above. The topic for the post is the installation of a technology that virtually allows fans to see the field from any seat in the house.

The insight for the post might include a link for fans to test the technology. The truth component might include what the features *can and cannot do* for fans wanting to use it online. The value for the reader might be getting a sneak preview of the technology before it is fully integrated into the main website. A unique perspective might include a video of the company filming the arena from many different angles, illustrating the behind-the-scenes aspects of developing the new technology. Want to make readers return to the site? At the end of the blog, tease them about what the next post will be.

Determining Frequency

Another question you may have is, "how often do I post?" Developing a consistent schedule for writing will not only help you manage your time, but it will also help define the reader's expectations.

If you write a handful of blog posts and then vanish for two months, readers will stop checking the blog and you'll lose all the work you've done to build up a fan base. If you post once or twice a week, however, readers will see that you have something to say on a consistent basis. Part of what you need to do is to manage the expectations of the readers and show consistency in posting. The more often you post fresh content, the better the chances you have for readers to return more often.

Built-in systems are available that allow you to schedule postings in advance that will appear on a pre-determined date and time. For example, each WordPress account includes a standard plug-in that allows you to set the date and time for each post to go live. Therefore, if you have completed your research, writing, editing, and scheduling, you can write several posts in one day and then automatically space them out to create fresh content over several days.

Developing an Editorial Calendar

After you have established a schedule for posting, you may want to consider developing an editorial calendar. This general guide will determine what will be written on any given day. For example, let's say your volleyball organization wants to develop a blog about men's and women's professional volleyball. The website already includes player profiles, photos, the schedule for the coming year, news releases, sponsorship, and purchasing information. These are typical items included on most sports websites.

The next step to consider is, what are you going to write about? Do you want to educate people about the rules of volleyball, provide insight into the training techniques the top players undertake in the off-season, explain why the latest promotional schedule is truly unique, recount the history of the sport or your organization? Will you consider feature stories on specific players, write about new sponsorship deals, or voice your opinion on the latest trends? These are all important topics, but unless you set up some sort of schedule, you may feel lost about what to write when or you may cover one topic too often.

You can create an editorial calendar by the week, month, and year. It can serve as your guide to what topics you plan to cover at a certain time and will help you focus on a specific area. For example, feature stories might appear on Mondays and Thursdays, educational posts on Tuesdays, and historical material on Wednesdays. The schedule may call for interviews with coaches, players, or avid fans to be posted on Fridays, while breaking news could happen at any moment. The need for an editorial calendar applies to a blog created for a team site or any type of organizational site.

Creating a Blogroll

An important aspect of a blog are its links to other related websites of interest. Often these links are listed in a hot links section called a *blogroll*. A site's blogroll is usually found on the right-hand side or at the bottom of a page. The information may be one long list of links or it may be divided into subcategories. Exhibit 4.6 shows the blogroll from the Businessofsports.com website; it includes links to industry-related websites, other popular blogs, and sport job sites, among others.

A blogroll is also an important tool for strategic linking. Search engines such as Google and Bing use sophisticated algorithms to determine just how popular or important a website or blog is. The bottom line is, the more websites and or blogs that are linked to yours, the higher your

EXHIBIT 4.6 The Business of Sports blogroll.

Source: http://www.thebusinessofsports.com/, January 25, 2013.

ranking of importance within a particular search engine. Search engines place an emphasis on incoming links to your blog. So, if you are willing to post a link to another site (an outbound link), it is just as important to ask them to link back to your site (an inbound link).

MARKETING THE BLOG ONLINE

While it would be nice to sit back and wait for readers to discover your blog, most will not just stumble onto your posts. Instead, an organization needs to market the blog, create visibility for each post online, and work to drive traffic to its URL address. You can help guide readers to your blog in many ways. Tactics you may want to consider include:

- Developing a regularly scheduled email blast to your database, creating story previews and links to specific blog posts.

- Promoting the blog link within your company's email signatures with direct links to the blog.

- Creating a link to the home page of the blog within selected press releases that are distributed to wide audiences.

- Linking each post to the organization's social media platforms as soon as it goes live. (Discussed in more detail later.)

- Posting a link to your latest blog entry within a targeted group on the business networking website LinkedIn and encouraging members to make comments on it.

- Encouraging posts by guest bloggers and asking them to promote the post to their audience via their own online communities such as Google+ or LinkedIn.

Using Plug-Ins

As mentioned earlier, blog publishing platforms have the advantage of plug-ins, which can make your site more effective. A popular plug-in called "All in One SEO" helps populate social media platforms like Facebook with appropriate headlines, descriptions, and tags when blog URLs are linked to it. All in One SEO is a simple free plug-in you can add to the administration portion of the blog (Exhibit 4.7).

EXHIBIT 4.7   All in One SEO.

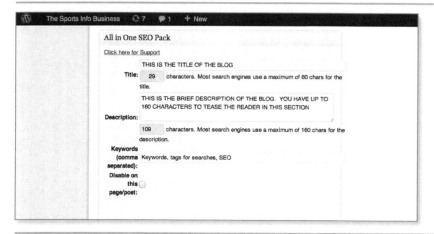

As shown in Exhibit 4.7, the All in One SEO Pack includes three areas that need to be filled out with each post. The first field is the title of the post. Typically, you would fill this section in with the title you have already created for the post. The second area is the description. You have 160 characters to describe the post and why your network should read it. When linking the posts to Facebook, this description, along with any photos you embed in the post, will be seen by Facebook friends or fans. Finally, there are keywords. This section, made up of keywords within your blog entry, helps readers find your post when they use search engines. The search engines index the keywords entered in this area and can help drive traffic to your site.

Additionally, imbedded plug-ins (such as AddThis), can populate each blog entry and help visitors to the site share the post by linking it with the most popular social media platforms. Using a plug-in like the one shown in Exhibit 4.8, if readers have enjoyed your post and want to share it with their Twitter followers, for example, if they click on the Twitter logo, a permission-based link appears in the users' feed.

Marketing Through Linking and Commenting

Not everyone is checking your blog every day to see if you have posted a new topic. However, by linking the post to other places where people follow your content, you are letting them know that something new

EXHIBIT 4.8   The plug-in AddThis.

has been posted. This is an easy way to remind people to come back and see what new perspective you have to share with others.

Make sure to develop inbound and outbound links that are connected to your site. These links, found in a sidebar section of the page as in a blogroll, serve as recommendations for other sites that you think will be relevant or interesting to your readers. As stated previously, search engines also place a value how many inbound and outbound links you have. The more inbound links that send people back to your site, the more important your website is perceived to be by the search engines.

You may also cross-promote your content on other social media platforms where like-minded users congregate. This includes popular sites such as Digg, Tumblr, StumbleUpon, and Reddit. Each of these sites allows you to post a link so that other people can accept your suggestions and click on the information.

Yet another way to create visibility for your blog is to post public comments on another person's blog entry and connect your name as an editor of a specific blog. Let's say your company is in the action sports industry, and you create insightful and fun content for this sport segment. One way to gain additional visibility is to regularly read and comment on the ESPN X Games site, where action sports live. Since this is one of the premiere television-based programming outlets for the action sports industry, your published comments along with your name, title, and company may inspire readers to click over and read your blog. Be careful not to come across as too self-serving by mentioning your blog within the comments, but linking it to your name and signature at the bottom of the comments is not perceived as offensive. It is a simple yet popular tool to drive traffic to your website.

Marketing Through Facebook

Finally, one last suggestion is to create a dedicated Facebook page for your organization if you have not already done so. Naturally, you will want to use the space to promote events, promotions, and ticket information. But by also linking to new blog content when it is fresh, fans will have a direct link back to the blog.

Take for example the Los Angeles Angels of Anaheim, which has a dedicated Facebook page. As of January 2013, the page had more than 530,000 fans (see Exhibit 4.9). One link to a blog post on that Facebook page could theoretically drive thousands of users to the blog and perhaps onto others once they find interesting content.

EXHIBIT 4.9   Los Angeles Angels' Facebook page.

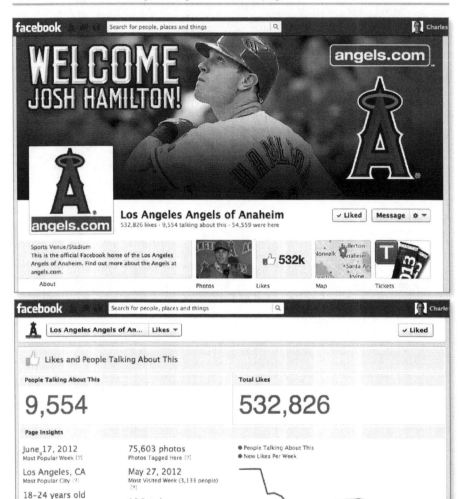

Source: www.facebook.com/LosAngelesAngels.

MEASUREMENT

Just as with a regular website, an independent blog can use the same analytics tools to teach bloggers about their readers. One of the easiest ways to measure a blog's statistics is to use a free tool called Google Analytics. In order to access this data, visit google.com/

EXHIBIT 4.10   Google Analytics Dashboard showing page visits by week.

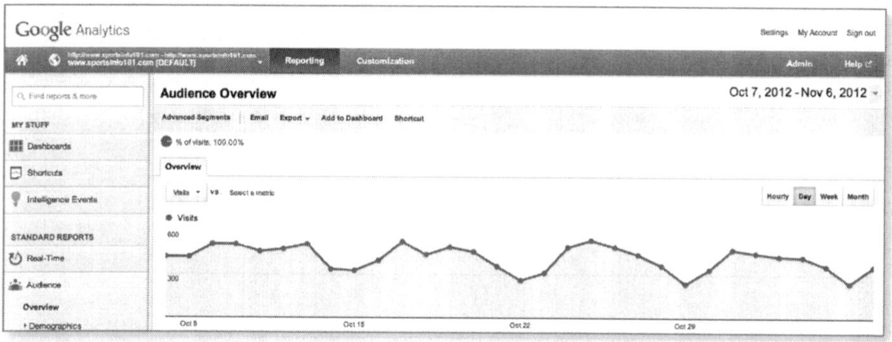

Google and the Google logo are registered trademarks of Google Inc., used with permission.

analytics and follow the simple directions (link to a website, copy a small bit of code, and place it on your own blog site). Once you've done this, you can learn how many people visit your site on any given day (see Exhibit 4.10).

This free tool can also help you gauge how many page views you have received, how long visitors spent on your site, as well as what parts of the world they come from, down to their city. This insight can help guide you when determining which content worked, who saw it, and how long they stayed on the site. If the story works, you may consider writing more like it. If no one reads the story, then you may learn that either the topic or the direction needs to change.

Once your blog has established a consistent and growing number of visitors, you may want to consider using free advertising services such as Google ads within the blog. These advertisements pay you, the blogger, money based on the number of people who click to view the content listed in the ads. The more traffic you have on the blog, the larger the audience and the better chances more people will click on the ad links, which means more income for you.

Chapter 9 discusses both website analytics and online advertising services in more detail.

CONCLUSION

logging is an effective tool that allows users to write and publish interesting content. There are a variety of free and paid platforms that teams as well as individuals can use. Regular, compelling blog posts keep readers interested, and creating and sticking to an editorial calendar will help establish reader expectations and guide the writing team on which topics to cover. Finally, there are effective free Internet tools that can help measure the reader's involvement with the blog. This feedback is invaluable in determining which content is most effective.

REVIEW QUESTIONS

1. Describe how blogging can increase traffic to your website.

2. What are characteristics of a good blog post?

3. What are the advantages and disadvantages to providing links within a story?

4. Compare the content and other aspects of two blogs from two sport organizations. How much time did you want to spend on each site? Did you click on any additional content? Which of the two blogs do you think is more effective?

5. Pick a subject to blog about. Research the topic, write a piece, and submit it to a sport blog for publication.

REFERENCES

Blogs. Retrieved from http://hub.uchicago.edu/guide/blogs#software.

Check page rank of web site pages instantly. (2012, Dec. 10). Retrieved from http://www.prchecker.info/check_page_rank.php.

eMarketer.com (2010, Aug.). U.S. Blog Readers, 2008–2014. Retrieved from http://www.emarketer.com/Article/Continued-Rise-of-Blogging/1007941.

Technorati.com (2012, Dec. 10). Sports blogs. Retrieved from http://technorati.com/blogs/directory/sports.

Thompson, C. (2006, Feb. 12). The Early Years. *New York Magazine*. Retrieved from http://nymag.com/news/media/15971/.

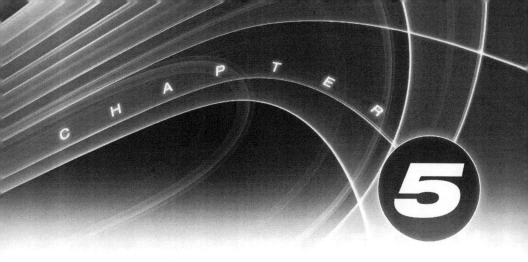

Photos, Video, and Podcasting

INTRODUCTION

A successful social media campaign involves many different components. While Facebook, YouTube, and Twitter remain integral components to any social media campaign, other ancillary sites can help make your social media campaign a sustained success.

Sites and services like Flickr, Instagram, and Ustream.tv play important roles in social media because they fill the gap between organization-created content (such as Facebook and Twitter) and user-created multimedia content (photos, videos) that users upload as they interact with your brand. These sites allow them to do just that.

In this age of social media and user-created content, it isn't enough for a brand to rely simply on the content it posts on its Facebook page or website. Organizations, especially those in the sport industry, increasingly rely upon their customers, fans, and audience to upload photos and videos and share them with others online. This action enhances an organization's messages by tapping into fan enthusiasm. Think of your fans or audience as brand ambassadors each time they share photos or stories from recent games with other fans.

In this chapter we examine how and why these sites play such an important role in successful social campaigns and how organizations can use them to achieve their goals. The chapter is divided into core categories: photos, video (including live streaming), and podcasts, each of which plays an important role in social media marketing.

PHOTOS

Photos have been a part of the Internet almost since its inception, but the use of photos on social networking sites has grown exponentially since 2007 or so. Online photo-sharing has exploded in popularity for three reasons: the proliferation of camera phones, the ubiquity of cheap online storage space and, most importantly, the social element of photo-sharing. Users want their friends and family to see their photos and share their experiences across the miles. This multimedia connection is a major force in social media.

Photo-Sharing Methods

Facebook users uploaded 250 million photos to the site each day as of 2012. The number has risen steadily over the years with the growing ubiquity of smartphones. Indeed, Facebook has more than 425 million users who access the site from their mobile devices.

The ease and popularity of sharing photos on Facebook isn't just limited to individuals, however. Organizations can utilize photo-sharing via Facebook as a way of reaching their audience. For example, an organization can create a custom tab with photo content and then ask users to comment on or share the featured photos. This tactic can turn a simple photo gallery into an interactive brand experience. In these instances, the audience is sharing in the "experience" of a brand rather than simply posting a "hey, love your brand!" message on the brand's page. This interactive element keeps visitors on the organization's Facebook page, thereby exposing them to your latest sales and promotions. Photo-sharing on Facebook continues to evolve as the site evolves.

Online photo-sharing isn't limited to just Facebook, however. Flickr remains one of the most popular photo-sharing sites in the world. The Yahoo!-owned site surpassed five billion user-uploaded images in September 2010, according to the official Flickr blog (Sheppard, 2010). Flickr differs from Facebook in that its photos can be shared easily with the larger Flickr community, whereas Facebook photos remain visible only to a select group, the user's friends.

On Flickr, users can sign up for two types of accounts: free accounts and pro accounts, the latter of which is a premium option. Users who opt for free accounts are limited in how many photos they can upload to Flickr each month and can only view their 200 most recent uploads. Pro users may upload unlimited photos of any size and view them all at a cost of approximately $25 per year.

Despite Flickr's two account types, the site's users interact with each other in one of the web's most vibrant online photo-sharing communities. Users of both types may create or join groups filled with photos and take part in discussions on a wide variety of topics. While Facebook does have groups, Flickr places a much larger emphasis on photos as the central feature of its groups.

Let's look at the differences between sharing photos via Facebook and Flickr from a marketing perspective. On Facebook, users upload photos that are attached to their account and categorized into galleries. In order to share them with a brand page, a user must either tag the brand in the photo or post it to the brand's wall. On Flickr users upload photos that are tied to their account, but the process of sharing photos with others is different—and this is a key distinction between the two sites.

On Flickr tags help other users find photos, in contrast to Facebook, where tagged photos are visible only to a user's friends. For example, if I take a photo of the Los Angeles Kings and tag it with "Los Angeles," "hockey," and the player's name, it will be easier for anyone searching Flickr to find my photo by searching with any of those tags. Therefore, more tags are better because it means more visibility for your picture or post (this strategy works for blog posts, too). The inherent openness of Flickr is a key difference from Facebook. By default, anyone can see photos posted to Flickr (you must make your account private to turn this feature off), whereas on Facebook only your friends can see your photos (and even then, you can change your settings to choose which friends see which photos).

In terms of photo-sharing, Facebook lends itself more to conversation surrounding photos with a central theme, say photos in a gallery. On Flickr, photos are shared publicly or in groups, but ultimately comments are tied to individual photos—not groups, like on Facebook. This may be one reason why Facebook is now the largest photo-sharing social site in the world. Its users are already on Facebook to connect with people; uploading their photos and sharing them is just an extension of this connection. Flickr is more of a dedicated photo site with communal features. Flickr is a destination site; Facebook is a portal site to all things social.

In April 2012, Facebook solidified its presence in the photo-sharing world by purchasing Instagram, the iOS and Android photo-sharing app (and access to its vibrant user community) for approximately $1 billion in cash (Rusli, 2012). Instagram began as a photo-sharing/editing application with heavy social elements. Users take or upload photos directly from their iPhones, iPads, or iPods and then place various filters on their photos, often with dramatic and interesting effects.

After uploading photos, users tag their photos with keywords and share them with friends from Facebook, their contacts list, and other users across Instagram. The result was a runaway hit for Instagram and, later, a billion-dollar payday and new positions at Facebook for its staff.

As smartphone users take and upload photos to Instagram, Facebook, and Flickr, it is important to remember that photo-sharing isn't limited to these three sites/apps. Twitter itself remains a popular photo-sharing tool as well. For an example of how powerful Twitter can be as a photo-sharing medium, let's examine the case of the Carolina Panthers' "Panthers Purrsuit" contest (see the box on the facing page).

In order to examine photo-sharing on Twitter, Toronto-based social media agency Sysomos (Levine, 2011) ran a one-day study of all tweets on May 30, 2011. The study found that 1.25 percent of all tweets included a photo that had been uploaded to a third-party hosting site. Despite the small percentage, this total amounted to approximately 2.125 million tweets daily that linked to hosted photos. As Twitter continues to grow, so too will its popularity as a photo-sharing service, especially now that Twitter is giving users an easier way to upload their photos to the service.

Developing a Photo-Sharing Strategy

As with any social media venture, organizations must develop a strategy for photo and media sharing. Most organizations post photos in the social space for two reasons: engagement and sponsorship fulfillment. When an organization decides to increase its use of photo-sharing, it does so as a means to an end: If your fans are using photo-sharing, then you should be, too.

Carolina Panthers' Purrsuit

In October 2010, the NFL's Carolina Panthers created a unique social media contest that involved both their fans and their sponsors. The contest, called Panthers Purrsuit, was an *Amazing Race*–type game in which teams of two raced around greater Charlotte in pursuit of prizes. The entire event was shared via Twitter and Facebook and included a significant photo-sharing element.

The contest asked participating teams to travel from sponsor to sponsor and complete some task in order to move on to the next location, in a manner similar to *The Amazing Race* reality show. In some cases, the required task involved tweeting a photo of the team with a mascot, a show owner, or a related landmark. In others, it required tweeting or sharing an answer to a trivia question with friends and followers.

The contest was successful and unique because of the way it combined real, tangible tasks with the social element of tweeting photos and sharing the experience with others. The Panthers' sponsors were given a new method of fulfillment through social media and the contest participants were given the opportunity to win prizes, all while the Carolina Panthers received exposure for their corporate partners and as a brand.

Fan engagement

Your fans are likely uploading photos and talking about your brand whether you're a part of the conversation or not. A proactive organization that encourages fan participation through photo- and video-sharing is an organization that builds a better, stronger relationship with its fans.

For example, let's take a look at how sport organizations use fan photos in Facebook pages and Flickr groups. In both instances, they ask fans to upload and share pertinent photos with other fans. In the case of Facebook, the organization can ask fans to post photos to the page's wall. In the case of Flickr, the organization can ask fans to upload photos to a shared group. In both instances these uploaded photos, any comments, or a caption and the name of the uploader are visible to all.

This is a good way to involve fans in building a sense of community. In this case the fans are spreading your organization's message on your behalf. To be sure, however, organizations must still maintain ultimate control over the content fans post to their social networking sites. A social media coordinator, for example, can monitor posted photos and filter them before they go public. This is a necessary step for any organization involved in social media.

Of course, sharing photos online is not limited to an organization's Facebook wall or its Flickr stream. When we talk about photo-sharing, we're not just talking about users posting photos. We're also talking about you posting photos on behalf of your organization. This includes photos on the organization's official website, blog, or in the media. Any photos that come from or feature your organization online become a part of your online photo-sharing plan.

Sponsorship fulfillment

While fans usually are eager to share photos online, they aren't the only segment a sport organization needs to think about when implementing a photo-sharing social media strategy. Sport marketers should also consider how photo-sharing can benefit their sponsors and their organization.

When Danica Patrick joined Twitter in February 2009, she did so at the behest of Tissot, the Swiss watchmaker that is one of her largest sponsors. Although many of her fellow IndyCar drivers were already on Twitter, Patrick had held off so her belated presence on the site was notable.

As part of her agreement with Tissot, Patrick tweeted to her thousands of followers photos of herself wearing a diamond-encrusted Tissot Heritage Prince watch and links to Tissot watches. The resulting exposure for the Tissot brand from a brand ambassador like Danica Patrick was valuable because it reached her diehard fans as well as a group of people more likely to buy a Tissot watch due to its endorsement from their favorite IndyCar driver.

In this example, the athlete is sharing photos for the purpose of promoting a sponsor's product, in this case a watch. But the beauty of the smartphone era is that anyone with a camera can share a photo with anyone else, albeit with a much smaller audience than a famous professional race car driver.

Most fans attending a game or an event at your venue are likely to have cell phones with cameras and Internet capability. This means your fans have an easy means of sharing photos online on behalf of your brand. This combination can mean big things to an organization with a strong Facebook and Flickr photo-sharing presence.

How can incorporating photo-sharing into a contest lead to better exposure for your brand? Let's say, for example, that you encourage fans to post photos of themselves enjoying their night at your venue, their kids enjoying the food, and even the promotions throughout the night.

These photos become testimonials to your brand. Your organization can achieve greater brand awareness by asking fans to share these photos on your Facebook page or Flickr group. The key here is to have fans tag their photos (through Facebook or Flickr) as memories from their visit to your stadium or venue so that others may find the photos very easily. This kind of grassroots marketing is prevalent in social media every day and is an easy way for brands to gain more exposure.

Your organization can select the best photos or have fans choose them from a group. You could feature the winners on your website or perhaps even in your marketing materials. Your fans are competing with each other for visibility—and tacit approval from the organization. A photo-sharing contest accomplishes both.

Now that we've examined photo-sharing, let's take a look at video-sharing, which has also exploded at an incredible rate in the past few years.

VIDEO

Online video-sharing has grown steadily since YouTube exploded onto the scene in 2005. A 2012 survey by Burson-Marsteller (2012) found that 79 percent of Global *Fortune* 100 companies are now on You-Tube, compared with 57 percent of companies just one year earlier.

Burson-Marsteller has conducted the "Global Social Media Checkup" survey annually since 2010, and the changes since then are eye-opening, especially in the way that these companies use social media. In 2010, Burson-Marsteller found that 79 percent of Global *Fortune* 100 companies maintained an official presence on at least one social media site (between Facebook, Twitter, and YouTube), overwhelmingly using that presence to broadcast corporate messages, while more or less ignoring users. In 2011, Burson-Marsteller concluded that these same companies took their presence on social sites to the next step by being more interactive and, indeed, having conversations with users on the sites. The study found that 67 percent of companies had replied to users on Twitter with an @ reply and 57 percent of companies had replied on Facebook. In 2012, the number of companies replying to Twitter users jumped to 79 percent, and companies were replying to Facebook users 70 percent of the time.

While *Fortune* 100 companies are already using online video, the sport industry's usage is growing steadily, too. Teams, leagues, and other sport organizations are generating content at an incredible rate—quality content at that—and audiences are clamoring for more video and more access to their favorite players and teams. Take, for example, the case of NBC's *Football Night in America*, one of the most watched weekly television programs each fall for the last 20 years.

"Sunday Night Football Extra" is the "companion arm" to the NBC broadcast. With "Sunday Night Football Extra," fans have the option of watching the Sunday Night Football game on their computers, iOS or Android smartphones, or tablets. This format offers fans an interactive experience with multiple camera angles, access to extra statistics, and the ability to chat with other fans through Twitter. Fans can watch the television broadcast as well as a handful of additional camera angles, including cameras isolated on star players from both teams, and read up-to-the-minute stats from that night's game. The enhanced broadcast element rewards fan engagement and extends the SNF brand beyond the television broadcast.

While NBC obviously has much greater pull online than a small organization or an individual account, the power of YouTube is its ability to spotlight products or ideas that may never have been discovered otherwise (as countless numbers of amateur-turned-professional YouTube singers can attest).

One of the most common and popular uses for YouTube is as a repository for customer testimonials. Take the case of SquareTrade, for example.

As we know, creativity in social media is often rewarded. Let's take a minute to review just how a small- or medium-sized organization could use video content on YouTube or another site to make an impact with its audience.

Tips for Using Video to Make an Impact

Identify the video footage that you want to upload

This may sound obvious, but it is imperative to identify content that will "play well" to online audiences. This means relevant, current content that clearly ties in with what your organization does. Older footage, for example, rarely has an impact unless it contains something rare or unseen before. Given the ubiquity of camera phones and video-editing software, it should be easy for an organization to film footage and place it online in a day or so, often much sooner.

SquareTrade, YouTube, & the Power of the People

SquareTrade is an Internet-only company that specializes in warranties for personal electronics such as laptops, TVs, e-readers, and the like. Founded in 1999, SquareTrade offers extended warranties at steep discounts over similar warranties at brick and mortar stores.

In a contest on YouTube, SquareTrade asked participants to upload a brief, two-minute video testimonial explaining why they recommend SquareTrade to their family and friends. The company then collected the YouTube videos and placed them in a custom tab on their Facebook page titled "Customers Speak." These testimonials do a better job selling SquareTrade warranties than any website or list of awards won by the company. In addition to featuring the videos on their Facebook page, SquareTrade awarded each participant with a free SquareTrade warranty, further increasing the likelihood that participants will recommend SquareTrade's services to their family and friends.

The SquareTrade YouTube contest is an example of how one small company adopted the "person on the street" testimonial to their benefit in the age of social media.

Edit the content to a suitable length

As noted earlier in this chapter, shorter videos are better when it comes to social media. Rather than uploading a single six- or seven-minute video, for example, uploading six separate one-minute videos is a better idea. Why? Shorter videos hook more viewers and are easier to share. In the YouTube age, every content publisher is fighting for attention from an audience that is only a click away from leaving your video.

While the content or the message of the video is always its most important factor, a shorter video is more desirable. Nearly 50 percent of all viewers drop off after a video's first minute (Adobe Scene7, 2010). As a result, a successful online video must hook its audience in less than 60 seconds. A shorter video is also more likely to be shared virally because of its immediate payoff—it gets right to the point.

Shorter online videos are also highly desirable for another reason: They translate into more videos. Although the original source video may be several minutes in length (an in-stadium interview, for example), the same video can provide fresh content on a team's blog for nearly a week if it is split up into shorter segments. Remember that original content is what keeps fans coming back to your blog or Facebook page.

Add tags

After you've edited your video down to an appropriate length, you owe it to your organization and fans to make it as easy to find as possible. Once again, this is done through tags or keywords. For example, if I film myself following a recipe for lasagna, I'd tag the video with words like *lasagna, Italian, cooking, dinner, recipe, how to, instructions, sauce,* and others. Obviously, the words *lasagna* and *recipe* will be in the title of the video, but these tags will point users to my video each time a user searches on one as a keyword.

Promote your video through social media

Too often organizations publish content and publicize it immediately across all social networks in one initial burst. Unfortunately, this method rarely proves effective because, in essence, you're shouting to everyone across every channel all at the same time. This is one example of why having a content publication schedule is a necessity when using social media these days. If you post your video to YouTube on day one, go ahead and tweet a link. But then wait a few days before you post it on your Facebook page. By waiting, you ensure that you won't over-saturate your audience with the same link repeatedly, and besides, by varying when you post your link you can reach a different audience.

While the most important part of publishing online video is having engaging content, organizations can really make their video work for them by promoting it in smart, effective ways that maximize its exposure.

Video Sources

Live streaming

Online video-sharing through social media extends beyond YouTube. In recent years live streaming video has taken off in its own right. Live streaming has made it possible for fans to get closer to their favorite athletes than ever before. Indeed, this phenomenon has allowed the athletes that embrace it to build their personal brands at an exponential rate.

Live streaming refers to the process by which a person (for example, a well-known athlete) streams live video directly from their computer's webcam through a free service such as Livestream or Ustream.tv. This allows athletes and fans to connect directly and immediately, without the filter of a team's public relations department or even the traditional media determining what fans can or cannot see. The setup takes mere minutes, making it even easier for athletes to tweet that they're going to be hosting a live chat and then beginning the chat at their convenience.

The immediate nature of live streaming is both good and bad for the athlete and organization. At its best, the medium offers unrestricted access to an athlete or organization, thus generating fan interest and involvement. At its worst, the unrestricted and unfiltered access can result in negative media coverage. The box below gives an example of how social media—and particularly live streaming—can have damaging side effects for athletes who act impulsively and foolishly when the world is listening.

While live streaming continues to be a tool primarily used by individual athletes, teams remain involved in other kinds of online video. The YouTube era has given rise to teams that produce their own original video content in house, without ever contacting a digital advertising or marketing agency.

Boxer Floyd Mayweather, Jr., on Ustream

In September 2010, famed boxer Floyd Mayweather, Jr. made headlines for all the wrong reasons when he used Ustream.tv to launch a live rant at rival Manny Pacquiao that was considered racist and homophobic. For years, the boxing community clamored to see top fighters Mayweather and Pacquiao step into the ring against each other. Indeed, speculation remained rampant that a "mega fight" between the two was in the cards throughout the summer of 2010, and yet the two never fought.

Allegedly, representatives from both boxers' camps were working to reach an agreement on a fight, but it fell through in late 2010. Rumor had it that a fight was agreed upon but Mayweather refused to sign off on it. It was clear that Mayweather had grown frustrated with Pacquiao throughout the months-long process.

Mayweather's frustration spilled over to anger and rage during a Ustream session with fans in September 2010. On the morning of September 2, Mayweather chatted with fans and during the session he repeatedly used ethnic and homophobic slurs when referring to Pacquiao. He told fans that he would "cook that little yellow chump" and would have Pacquiao "make me some sushi rolls and cook some rice."

Mayweather was universally condemned for his actions (Cofield, 2010), and a fight with Pacquiao never materialized. Thus, Mayweather became a prime example of the ways social media can connect athletes with fans and the possible negative consequences contained therein.

In-house video

Because organizations have the power to create in-house video content, as you will see in a moment with the Timberwolves and Giants, the sky's the limit when it comes to publishing unique and engaging video content to your social channels. Organizations no longer need thousand-dollar software suites to edit materials together; most can get by with Apple's iMovie or a similar program that is available for free or at a low cost. And as the availability of quality video cameras, phones, and other portable devices has increased, it has become even easier to shoot some quick footage, edit it on a computer, and upload it in a matter of minutes.

It is this ease of access and of use that makes in-house production a growing trend in the sport industry. To be sure, there are still plenty of opportunities for an organization to hire an outside agency to build traditional television advertising campaigns, but the rules have changed for shorter quality content in the age of social media.

The Minnesota Timberwolves are one of the NBA's most social media–friendly franchises. Despite not posting a winning record since the 2004–05 NBA season, the Timberwolves have made headlines for their creative use of YouTube and social media in promoting their team and players.

The Timberwolves have twice created spoof commercials for star forward Kevin Love. During Love's rookie season, the Timberwolves created a faux infomercial for "Kevin Love's Glass Cleaner," a tongue-in-cheek way of promoting Love's candidacy for the NBA Rookie of the Year Award. Although Love didn't win the award, the advertisement, which initially appeared only on the team's website and YouTube channel, gained widespread attention from ESPN and the sport blogosphere.

The Timberwolves created a second commercial and an accompanying website, www.612allstar.com, in support of Love's candidacy for the 2010–11 NBA All-Star Game. The commercial was viewed more than 117,000 times in its first week on YouTube. (The site no longer exists.)

The Minnesota Timberwolves are not the only pro sports team making an impact with YouTube. Indeed, a hockey team from Northern Ireland has also used online video to grow its brands. The Elite Ice Hockey League's Belfast Giants created a viral sensation, too, when they released a music video of the entire team lip-syncing to Mariah Carey's "All I Want for Christmas Is You" in December 2010 (http://www.youtube.com/watch?v=wzad9-Z0oTU). The video's real purpose was to promote a post-Christmas three-game homestand, but the video went viral on Twitter and Facebook in a matter of hours.

While the Belfast Giants succeeded in creating a hit, the team made one costly mistake when promoting the video: They initially made it private on YouTube. A private video on YouTube does not appear in search results. The only way to view a private video is to access it through its direct link. Fans searching for "Belfast Giants music video" or "hockey team lip sync video" could not find it. The Giants lost hundreds—if not thousands—of views per day until the video was finally made public. Although the video went viral, it would have reached more people had it been public from the beginning.

Both the Minnesota Timberwolves and the Belfast Giants understand that the era of YouTube means that teams now have the ability to create and publish outstanding and original content entirely in house. What once cost thousands of dollars of an advertising budget can now be done for significantly less and much faster within their organization.

Fan-generated content

Although fan-generated photos can be on par with those taken professionally, fan-generated videos are often of a much lower quality than their professional counterparts. For example, when the Boston Bruins won the 2011 Stanley Cup, the team and the NHL posted many professional-quality videos on their websites along with an official DVD release of the Bruins' run to the Stanley Cup. During the Bruins Stanley Cup run, fans posted video montages of jarring hits and nifty goals set to heavy metal soundtracks. While the fans' hearts were in the right place by posting the content, the team itself was not responsible for the soundtracks, some of which included profanity. In this sense, fan-created videos can be more damaging to a brand than photos. Not all fan-created videos are bad, but the content must be vetted before it is added to any official team social account. In the long run a team can do little to prevent such content from appearing on personal accounts unless it infringes upon a copyright.

Creating Impact: What Makes a Video a Hit?

What makes a particular video popular while others go unviewed for weeks at a time? While there is no easy, catch-all answer, the simplest explanation is that successful videos are both creative and easy to find. Indeed, both the Timberwolves and Giants used creative videos to spread their messages and were rewarded with widespread exposure on the blogosphere.

A video becomes a viral hit in part because its reach extends beyond the organization's own general fanbase or audience. A fan tells another fan who tells another fan, who tweets the video link or shares it with friends on Facebook or Google+. Word of mouth drives social media. But what are key elements to successful online videos? Adobe published a report in late 2010 (Adobe Scene7, 2010) that delved into this topic. Adobe's research indicated that a successful online video must contain nine basic steps or elements. These are:

1. Choose your featured product wisely
2. Streamline production
3. Keep it short
4. Put the spotlight on your product
5. Make your videos visible
6. Optimize the video player
7. Make your video count
8. Make video accessible to consumers on the go
9. Choose a video platform designed with retailers in mind

Let's look at some key takeaways for each step as they pertain to the sports industry.

1. Choose your featured product wisely.   Ask yourself what you want to feature on your Facebook page or YouTube channel. What are you hoping to accomplish by featuring this content?

2. Streamline production.   With the right tools, organizations can create quality content in an hour if necessary. But in order to do this, it is imperative that an organization have a high-quality digital camera or camcorder at the ready to record content and then a high-quality, easy-to-use video editing program like Apple's iMovie or Microsoft Movie Maker to edit and post content quickly. This is what it means to streamline production.

3. Keep it short.   Once again: shorter videos have a greater impact on YouTube and in social channels. Get to the point quickly or your audience will move on to something else. Keep it short (and shareable).

4. Put the spotlight on your product.   If you are a nonprofit organization advertising an appearance by a star athlete at your event, make sure to promote the appearance and the event across all of your channels. Don't just tell your audience that the star player will be at the event, tell them all about the event and then mention the athlete's appearance as a "sweetener" to make attending even more attractive. Put the spotlight on your product.

5. Make your videos visible.   There are two simple rules for online video: Make it easy to find and to share your content across all social channels. If you post content to your YouTube channel, you should embed that same content on your official blog and on your Facebook profile. Tweet links to the video. Make your content highly visible and give your audience a chance to share it with others. Broaden your scope and reach as many as possible with a highly visible (and interesting) video.

6. Optimize the video player.   If you want to share content, the emphasis should be on the content and not the technology powering said content. One way to avoid technology headaches is to make sure you use YouTube, a widely known, easily accessible site with very little downtime thanks to the strength of Google's servers. YouTube also features easy tools so users can share or embed your content elsewhere, thereby increasing your reach.

7. Make your video count.   As we've established, shorter videos are better. Make your videos count. Get right to the point. If you're posting an interview, spend less time on a splashy introduction and more time on the interview subject and their answers. Remember, if your video is part of a larger series (say the first of five parts), tell your audience this at the end of every video and in the comments.

8. Make video accessible to consumers on the go.   In short, publish to YouTube and you won't have much trouble ensuring your video content is available on the go. The YouTube application is standard on all Apple and Android smartphones and tablets as of 2011.

9. Choose a video platform designed with retailers in mind.   This step may not apply to your organization. If it does, just remember that your content should ultimately sell your organization and your relationships with your sponsors, be they retailers or otherwise. In short, your content should always sell something.

Video remains an important part of an online marketing plan. While there's no magical recipe for success with online video, organizations that produce high-quality content on a regular basis and make it easily accessible are more likely to enjoy success than organizations that only upload new content on a monthly basis. The key is to publish original content and keep your fans coming back for more.

PODCASTS

A podcast is an audio or video recording created for and specifically distributed via the Internet. Podcasts have grown steadily in popularity in recent years. While self-produced podcasts have long been a staple of fan blogs, professionally produced podcasts are now the standard in the sport industry.

Television and radio stations were among the earliest adopters of podcasting technology. ESPN's "Pardon the Interruption" launched its popular podcast in April 2006 and remains one of the most listened to sports podcast available today. Other television and radio programs soon followed suit to varying degrees of success.

An audio podcast is often simply the audio of a radio show or audio-only portion of a television program. No matter what the format, a podcast's most important feature is its "on demand" nature and portability, both conveniences for today's busy users.

Major media organizations like CNN, NPR, and ESPN all maintain audio and video podcasts on their websites, available as free downloads

How to create your own podcast

Do you have access to a computer with a built-in webcam and microphone? Congratulations, you can now create your own podcasts! It is actually quite easy. Perhaps the most difficult aspect of creating a podcast is deciding what topic you'll discuss and the format the show will take.

In order to create a podcast, you can use your computer's built-in microphone or a headset with a built-in microphone or even a pair of smartphone earbuds if they include a microphone. A multitude of free or inexpensive applications are available for both PCs and Macs that allow you to record from your microphone directly to your computer. These programs record your podcast in MP3 format, which you may then post online immediately or edit as you see fit.

Once you've recorded a podcast (which can be as brief as a few minutes or as long as several hours), you can place it online in the iTunes store where anyone can find and download it for free. If you promote your podcast through social media as well, you can grow your audience over time. Technology has made it easy to make a podcast. It's up to you to decide what you want your podcast to be about—and what you want to say.

or via iTunes. The iTunes U section of iTunes also contains podcasts from colleges and universities across the country. This ease of access is one of the most convenient features of today's podcasts.

How are podcasts being used in the sport industry? While major media organizations such as ESPN offer podcasts of their sports shows, sport organizations are using podcasts in a similar manner yet on a smaller scale: they are using the convenience and portability of podcasts to reach a larger audience at a time when it's convenient for that audience. In short, podcasts are another way of spreading your brand beyond the walls of your stadium or arena.

For example, let's say that you work for a minor league baseball team that records one in-depth, 10-minute-long "getting to know you" interview with a different player on the team each week. Your organization can publish this podcast on its website and through iTunes, thereby making it easier for fans to find and listen to your content. This is a free and effective way of marketing your brand, too.

As we discussed in the video section earlier, shorter content is better, except when it comes to podcasts. Many popular podcasts are simply an audio version of television content (think ESPN's PTI), so many listeners are accustomed to podcasts longer than YouTube clips.

As with the other elements we've discussed, podcasts are just one part of a successful social media strategy. Podcasts alone do not represent strong social media engagement but are part of a successful strategy when used in conjunction with the other elements discussed in this book. In today's immediate "share now" social world, podcasts are still a part of online branding, albeit one that often takes a backseat to YouTube videos. Still, if your organization has a plethora of audio available, putting that content into a podcast is easy enough to do and represents yet another branding opportunity.

CONCLUSION

We've discussed ways organizations can use photos, online video, and podcasting to extend their reach beyond their official website and Facebook profile. Each of the methods discussed in this chapter are elements of an overall social media strategy. More and more organizations will use technology such as live streaming video and podcasts as the technology becomes easier to use. Yet it is important for a forward-thinking organization interested in marketing via social media to become comfortable with these technologies now so as to remain on the forefront of the new media marketing push.

REVIEW QUESTIONS

1. Name four of the largest social media channels in the United States.

2. What are the main differences between sharing photos on a social network such as Facebook versus a photo-sharing site such as Flickr? List at least two situations in which a sport organization would want to post photos on Facebook and two situations in which they would use Flickr.

3. What are four key elements of any online video? Why are these elements so important to a video's success?

4. Listen to three sport-related podcasts. What makes them effective or not? Did you recognize a message in any of them? How long are the podcasts and how often are new podcasts posted? Does this make you more or less likely to listen to them?

REFERENCES

Adobe Scene7 (2010). Nine easy steps to online video success. Retrieved from http://www.slideshare.net/E-M-3/nine-easy-steps-to-online-video-success.

Belfast Giants Hockey Team (2010). All I want for Christmas is you. Retrieved from http://www.youtube.com/watch?v=wzad9-Z0oTU.

Burson-Marsteller.com (2012). Global social media check-up 2012. Retrieved from http://www.burson-marsteller.com/social/infographic.aspx.

Cofield, S. (2010, Sept. 3). Mayweather's racial rant on Pacquiao crosses the line. Yahoo! Sports. Retrieved from http://sports.yahoo.com/box/blog/box_experts/post/Mayweather-s-racial-rant-on-Pacquiao-crosses-the?urn=box-267366.

Infographics Lab (2012, Feb. 15). Facebook 2012. Retrieved from http://infographiclabs.com/infographic/facebook-2012/.

Levine, S. (2011, June 2). How people currently share photos on Twitter. Retrieved from http://blog.sysomos.com/2011/06/02/how-people-currently-share-pictures-on-twitter/.

Mashable (2011, Feb.). How much do you know about Facebook photos? Retrieved from http://8.mshcdn.com/wp-content/uploads/2011/02/021111_02.png.

Patrick, D. (2010, July 3). Here's the Tissot Heritage Prince watch, love the diamonds! Retrieved from https://twitter.com/#!/DanicaPatrick/status/17678396524.

Rusli, E. M. (2012, April 9). Facebook buys Instagram for $1 billion. *New York Times*. Retrieved from http://dealbook.nytimes.com/2012/04/09/facebook-buys-instagram-for-1-billion/.

Sheppard, Z. (2010, Sept. 19). 5,000,000,000. Retrieved from http://blog.flickr.net/en/2010/09/19/5000000000/.

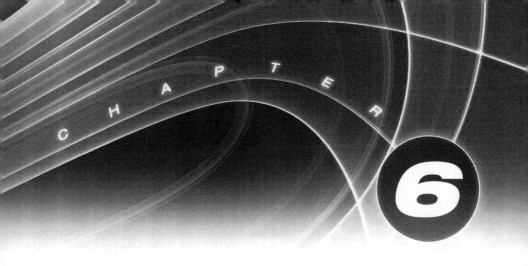

Search Marketing

INTRODUCTION

By now, you've learned how people use social media tools to find information about sports. However, fans aren't ignoring other ways to obtain information. Consumers still turn to search engines to help them find what they want. In this chapter, we'll discuss the importance of search engine marketing (SEM), which is defined as the practices used to improve the position of a website in search engine results pages (Website Marketing Services, n.d.).

As marketers, we must know how to help sport organizations reach their customers using the methods that their customers prefer. SEM offers many opportunities for organizations to get their brands, products, and services in front of people and to be there when people search for items that interest them. The search marketing industry is expanding, and a growing number of companies are investing time and money in this practice as part of their marketing plans. According to the State of Search Marketing Report 2011 from the Search Engine Marketing Professional Organization, the value of the North American search marketing industry grew 16 percent in 2011 to $19.3 billion, up from $16.6 billion in 2010 (Enright, 2011).

In this chapter we discuss the current search marketing landscape and why SEM is something that more sport organizations should be taking advantage of. We'll cover the two main tactics that make up search marketing—search engine optimization (SEO) and paid search, or pay-per-click (PPC)—and the benefits, key components, and strategy basics for each. We'll also go through some of the challenges associated with each of these key search marketing tactics.

SEARCH ENGINE MARKETING OVERVIEW

All of us have used search engines to find information on people, companies, athletes, and other topics of interests. But it's important to have a basic understanding of how search engines work before you can understand search engine marketing.

Search Engines and Results Pages

As you probably know, a search engine is a program that collects and organizes information about millions of web pages. Search engines create databases of websites based on many factors, including the pages' titles, keywords, and text. When someone visits a search engine, such as Google, and types in a keyword or phrase, the search engine returns the most relevant websites based on proprietary algorithms (the search engine's set of rules). These lists of results are referred to as search engine results pages (SERPs).

With many of the popular search engines, the SERPs yield a mix of web pages because of one or both of the following reasons:

1. The search engine's algorithm deems them to be most relevant to the keyword or phrase the person searched for. These results are often considered to be the "organic" or "natural" listings on SERPs.

2. A company has paid to show up in the results for the searcher's keyword or phrase. These results are often called the "paid" or "sponsored" listings on SERPs.

Exhibit 6.1 shows an example of organic and paid listings on a search engine results page for the phrase "sports ticket." According to a 2010 study by Performics, nearly two-thirds of Internet users know the difference between the paid and natural listings, with people ages 18 to 29 most likely to be aware of the difference (Performics, 2010). Both types of listings are important, as the study also found that about half of respondents are more likely to click on a search result if a company appears multiple times on the SERP.

EXHIBIT 6.1   Paid and organic listings on a SERP.

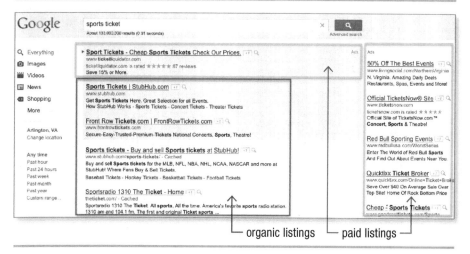

Google and the Google logo are registered trademarks of Google Inc., used with permission.

Major Search Engines

While there are hundreds of online search engines, the major players are Google, Microsoft's Bing, Yahoo! (which uses Bing to power their search results), and Ask. According to Compete's May 2011 Search Market Share Report (Han, 2011), Google received 64 percent of all U.S. searches, while Bing-powered searches accounted for 32 percent of all searches. Of Bing's share, Microsoft received 17 percent of these searches and Yahoo! 15 percent. Ask garnered a 4 percent share of searches. As marketers, it's important to keep an eye on these numbers to get an understanding of which search engines may be most valuable to include in an overall SEM plan.

These are the basics of SEM. Now let's discuss why sport marketers should care about it.

SEARCH ENGINE MARKETING IN SPORTS

The primary reason why sport marketers should embrace SEM is the same as the reason why they should be implementing social media programs: Their audiences are already utilizing these tools, and sport marketers need to be where their audiences are. Search engines are especially important in helping consumers find information that leads to purchase decisions. According to a study from GroupM and

Comscore, 58 percent of consumers start their purchase journey with an online search. In fact, 51 percent of consumers use online search alone in the buying process (Ramesh, 2011). This research shows that many fans may make purchase decisions for such items as tickets and merchandise solely based on information they find via search engines. If a sport organization does not show up in search results for keywords related to their products and services, they're likely missing out on potential sales and new customers.

This is especially important in selling tickets to individual games. Let's say a fan is interested in buying tickets to a Washington Nationals game. She may do an Internet search for "Washington Nationals tickets." If the team's website is not at or near the top of the SERP, she may never find it and instead purchase tickets from the site that is at the top of the search results. For the sake of this example, let's say this is a site like goodseattickets.com or vividseats.com, which both sell tickets to sport, musical, and theatrical events. If this happens, the team misses out on potential revenue in a few different ways:

- Partial lost revenue from the sale of the tickets, since the ticket site will take a percentage of the sale.

- Revenue from other items (e.g., T-shirts, hats, tickets to multiple games, etc.) that the fan might have purchased during this same shopping experience if she had visited your online store.

- Potential future revenue that may have come as a result of the fan visiting the team's website and opting to participate in the team's email marketing, mobile marketing, or social media marketing programs.

Another reason why sport marketers need to consider SEM is that search and social media often are used together by fans in the process of making purchase decisions. According to GroupM and Comscore, 40 percent of consumers who use a search in their path to purchase are motivated to use social media to continue their decision-making process (Ramesh, 2011). For example, someone may be looking to buy an instructional mixed–martial arts DVD. A search may reveal two or three companies that sell what he wants. The person might visit these companies' blogs, watch their videos on YouTube, and see what people are saying about them on Twitter before deciding which company to purchase from. Forty-eight percent of respondents combined search engines and social media in the buying process, and 30 percent of people reported that they use social media to eliminate brands from contention.

A final reason to understand SEM is that there are opportunities for agencies to help sport organizations and jobs for people who understand this space. As we mentioned, the SEM industry is growing and many companies are now outsourcing their SEM activities. The result is an increasing need for people and agencies who can skillfully apply SEM strategies and tactics.

SEM has the potential to help or hurt a sport organization's overall marketing efforts. In order to take full advantage of the process, sport marketers must have a solid understanding of its two main tactics—search engine optimization and paid search.

SEARCH ENGINE OPTIMIZATION (SEO)

SEM often involves complex tasks and research and specialized knowledge. We won't be able to cover all the ins and outs of SEM in this chapter, but we will offer a basic overview of what it is and why it's important. We'll spend a little more time on SEO than paid search, mainly because social media is becoming more tightly integrated with SEO than with paid search.

Let's start by exploring the essentials of SEO, which involves optimizing a website and its content so that it shows up in the organic, or natural, listings of SERPs.

SEO Overview

Search engines utilize a complex variety of factors in their algorithms to decide that a certain web page is relevant for a specific keyword search and where that web page will appear in the results. SEO consists of understanding how these algorithms and rules work and then utilizing tactics to help websites show up in the organic listings of SERPs, especially for specific keywords that drive website traffic. To simplify, SEO helps a website prove its relevance to a search engine and get more traffic for related keywords. However, driving traffic is only one part of SEO; as we'll discuss later in the chapter, ranking for the right keywords is vital to ensure that rankings lead to actions, such as purchases, email signups, and donations.

Successful SEO offers benefits. The first is that it can be very cost effective compared with paid search. With SEO, companies don't pay for each click to their website, like they do with paid search (i.e., PPC). Effective SEO efforts can be a great source of profitable traffic.

In addition to usually being less expensive than PPC campaigns, SEO can help marketers gain higher conversion rates than they may receive through PPC campaigns. Conversion rate is calculated by taking the number of people who complete a desired action, such as a purchase, and dividing it by the number of people who viewed a website or specific page of a website. According to a study from MarketingSherpa, organic search traffic delivers higher conversion rates than PPC traffic (Doyle, 2010). For example, the conversion rate for a company's PPC campaigns may be 2 percent, but the conversion rate for people who find the site in the natural search results (due to the company's SEO efforts) may be 5 percent. This holds true across all types of conversions, including online sales and leads generated.

Another benefit of SEO is that it provides companies with multiple branding opportunities within the SERPs. For example, typically ten web pages (plus images, and sometimes videos) appear on the first page of the search results. With the right approach to SEO, a team or organization may be able to "own" some or all of the spaces on this page. This gives the organization countless more branding and traffic opportunities than if it appears only once in the listings.

Social media often plays a big part in SEO success as an organization's social media presence often appears on the first page of the SERPs and is usually listed as a separate entry. Exhibit 6.2 shows an example of the exposure that Red Bull receives for its own content (when the search term is "red bull") due to its SEO and social media efforts, compared to 5-hour Energy (when the search term is "five hour energy").

As you can see in Exhibit 6.2, Red Bull controls seven listings on the first page of the Google results for the search query "red bull." Their social media efforts play a key role in this, as their Facebook, Twitter, and YouTube profile pages all show up here. Overall, this gives Red Bull many more opportunities to gain website traffic and sales than if they only appeared once or twice in the listings. Compare that to the listings for 5-hour Energy. On the first page of listings, only the first two results point to content that was created by the company; the rest are other organizations' messages about the drink.

According to the "2011 Social Media Marketing Report" from Social Media Examiner, 71 percent of marketers who use social media plan to increase their use of SEO in the near future (Stelzner, 2011). Social media and SEO are becoming more integrated, especially as search engines refine their algorithms to personalize search results. For example, Bing now brings information from Facebook friends into

EXHIBIT 6.2 Comparing Red Bull and 5-hour Energy social media presences.

---

red bull   ✕ | Search

About 146,000,000 results (0.07 seconds)   Advanced search

➡ ▶ **Red Bull.com -- Red Bull** 🔍
Red Bull.com International delivers info on Red Bull events, videos, photos, Web TV and the
latest news on Red Bull athletes, teams, and music.
Products & Company - Videos - Contact Us - Events
www.redbull.com/ - Cached - Similar

Red Bull - Wikipedia, the free encyclopedia 🔍
Red Bull is an energy drink sold by the Austrian Red Bull GmbH. It was created in 1987 by
the Austrian entrepreneur Dietrich Mateschitz and on market share, ...
Taurine - Dietrich Mateschitz - Red Bull Racing - Vodka Red Bull
en.wikipedia.org/wiki/Red_Bull - Cached - Similar

➡ **Red Bull USA - Sports & Entertainment News | Teams & Athletes ...** 🔍
1 day ago - Get info on Red Bull events, videos, photos, and the latest news on Red Bull
athletes, teams, and music. Red Bull Energy Drink - Red Bull ...
www.redbullusa.com/ - Cached - Similar

News for red bull

  Supporters to Give Red Bulls the Silent Treatment 🔍
3 hours ago
By JACK BELL Todd Heisler/ The New York TimesNormally vocal Red Bulls fans in the
South Ward section of Red Bull Arena plan to go silent in a protest ...
New York Times (blog) - 11 related articles
Red Bull's Webber on pole for German GP 🔍
AFP - 1187 related articles
Elated Hamilton surprised by McLaren pace 🔍
AFP - 431 related articles

Images for red bull - Report images

➡ **Red Bull | Facebook** 🔍
Red Bull - Red Bull Gives You Wiings. So does the RedBulletin.com | Facebook.
www.facebook.com/redbull - Cached - Similar

➡ **Red Bull (redbull) on Twitter** 🔍
Red Bull (redbull) is on Twitter. Sign up for Twitter to follow Red Bull (redbull) and get their
latest updates.
twitter.com/redbull - Cached - Similar

What's Inside: Red Bull 🔍
Jun 26, 2007 – Like most popular soft drinks, Red Bull is largely sugar water. But don't count
on its glucose to "give you wings," as the ad says. ...
www.wired.com/science/discoveries/magazine/15.../st_redbull - Cached - Similar

➡ **Red Bull Air Race** 🔍
An international competition based on speed and precision. Includes photographs, race
results, event schedule, pilot biographies, and details of manoeuvres.
www.redbullairrace.com/cs/.../Red-Bull.../001238611393596 - Cached - Similar

➡ **Red Bull Racing :: Red Bull** 🔍
6 hours ago - The official site with news, video, results and photos.
www.redbullracing.com/ - Cached - Similar

➡ **redbull's Channel - YouTube** 🔍
Road To Romania with Chris Birch - e6 - Red Bull Romaniacs 2011. 1681 views - 11 hours
ago ... MTB Track explanation - Red Bull Joyride 2011 - Crankworx ...
www.youtube.com/user/redbull - Cached - Similar

(continued)

EXHIBIT 6.2 Comparing presences, continued.

| five hour energy | 🎤 | 🔍 |

About 79,800,000 results (0.44 seconds)

➡ **5-hour ENERGY® Shots - No Sugar & Zero Net Carbs** 🔖
www.5hourenergy.com/
5-hour ENERGY® shots for long lasting energy with no sugar and zero net carbs.
→ Ingredients - Contact Us - FAQs - Original

➡ **What's in a 5-hour ENERGY® shot?** 🔖
www.5hourenergy.com/ingredients.asp
5-hour ENERGY® shots combine a unique blend of ingredients to provide you
with the energy you need when you need it.

5-hour Energy - Wikipedia, the free encyclopedia 🔖
en.wikipedia.org/wiki/5-hour_Energy
5-hour Energy (stylized as 5-hour ENERGY) is a flavored "energy shot" (energy
drink) made by Innovation Ventures. The product is manufactured in Farmington
...
→ Ingredients - Effectiveness - Warnings - Variations

Images for five hour energy - Report images

5 Hour Energy Review 🔖
www.consumerreports.org › Home › Health
Get a 5 hour energy review to find out if the claims about it are true from the
medical experts at Consumer Reports Health.

The Mystery Monk Making Billions With 5-Hour Energy - Forbes 🔖
www.forbes.com/.../manoj-bhargava-the-mystery-monk-making-billi...
Feb 8, 2012 – Ever heard of Manoj Bhargava? Probably not. He's a former monk
who struck it rich with that ubiquitous red bottle: 5-Hour Energy. Read his ...

Perks of Five-Hour Energy Put to Test - CBS News 🔖
www.cbsnews.com/2100-500165_162-7326410.html
Feb 9, 2011 – It's one tiny bottle that promises to pack a lot of energy. And with
an advertising budget of close to $90 million, the 5-hour Energy shot has ...

Amazon.com: 5-Hour Energy - Berry 1.93-Ounce Packages (Pack of ... 🔖
www.amazon.com › ... › Beverages › Energy Drinks
★★★★☆ Rating: 3.9 - 120 reviews - $23.94 - In stock
That's it. We'll automatically place your orders and deliver them to you at the
interval you select. Benefits. Get a discount on our everyday price; Pay for each ...

The Rise of the 5-Hour Energy Drink - NYTimes.com 🔖
well.blogs.nytimes.com/2012/.../the-rise-of-the-5-hour-energy-drink/
Feb 29, 2012 – A two-ounce caffeine and vitamin elixir that promises a five-hour
energy boost has become a $1 billion brand and is ever-present on store ...

EXHIBIT 6.3   Example of Google personalizing search results.

Google and the Google logo are registered trademarks of Google Inc., used with permission.

search results to display sites and pages they've liked that related to a specific search query (Bing Team, 2011). Google also has personalized results by indicating if Facebook friends have shared a page in the SERPs on Twitter or shared it with Google's +1 button (Fishkin, 2011). See Exhibit 6.3 for an example of how this feature appears.

As you can see, social media is already contributing to the personalization of organic search results. Social media likely will become even more important in influencing organic search rankings so it's important that marketers understand this and keep up with how this could impact SEO efforts.

Key Components of SEO

Sport marketers should be aware of three key SEO components:

1. Keywords
2. On-site factors
3. Links

Regardless of whether or not you ever directly manage SEO initiatives for a sport organization, knowing the basic components will keep you informed, especially as SEM and social media continue their convergence.

Keywords

As mentioned earlier, search engines use complex algorithms to determine where a website or page should rank in the organic listings for a keyword or variety of keywords. A user types a query into the search, such as "rugby season schedule" or "where can I buy rugby jerseys?" The search engine "sees" keywords and keyword phrases such as "rugby" and "buy jerseys." SEO dictates that certain words or phrases need to correspond with a company's content, products, and/or services. Sport organizations should want their websites to rank for keywords that are most relevant to the content on their sites and that deliver website visitors that are most likely to complete actions that the organization desires, such as making purchases or donations. For example, a youth baseball league in Charlotte, North Carolina, may wish to rank for a variety of main keywords or key phrases, including:

- Youth baseball Charlotte
- Charlotte kids baseball
- Youth baseball league Charlotte
- Charlotte kids baseball team

This example depicts some primary or top keywords that a company may seek to try to rank for. These main keywords can be very important; however, there may also be hundreds or thousands of secondary or "long-tail" keywords that a business may want to rank for (Krijestorac, 2010). Individually, these long-tail keywords may not have as many people searching for them or result in as much traffic as main keywords do. But collectively, these long-tail keywords may help a business drive even more traffic than main keywords. A golf club company might want to rank for the following long-tail keywords:

- How to choose the right golf clubs
- Golf club sizes for 14 year old
- Where to buy golf clubs near New York City
- Buying the right-sized golf clubs
- Finding golf clubs that fit

Ranking in SERPs for the right keywords is important to generating results with SEO. For example, let's say you're a company that sells autographed merchandise. Maybe you show up in search results pages on a search for "sports hat" and are getting a lot of website traffic from this search query. However, the people who are looking for sports hats probably aren't looking for autographed merchandise, so your traffic isn't converting well. It would be more important to rank for "autographed hat" instead.

Or, perhaps your company ranks number one for a keyword search on "autographed lacrosse jersey." However, not many people search for this term, so there is not much traffic to be gained from ranking number one in the SERPs. The above phrase may be a good long-tail keyword, but the company likely shouldn't make this the main keyword in its SEO efforts. Companies must choose keywords that they'd like to rank for AND that are relevant and will drive profitable traffic to their websites.

On-site factors

The second key component of SEO is the on-site factors that search engines use to help determine a website's or page's relevance for a given search query. In order for a website to maximize its rank for a given keyword, you can tweak it to signal the search engines that it is relevant to that keyword.

Unique and accurate page titles.   Page titles should include the keyword a company is trying to rank in searches for. For example, the site goodseattickets.com has the homepage title "Good Seat Tickets for Concert, Theatre, and Sport." However, businesses should utilize unique page titles for *each* page in their websites. For example, a website that sells baseball equipment may want to include "baseball equipment" and the company name in the page title of its homepage and "baseball gloves" on the pages with gloves, "baseball bats" on the bat page, and so on.

Heading tags.   Just as newspaper headlines alert readers to what an article is about, the H1 tag alerts search engines to what a page is about (Hare, 2009). This tag is a piece of HTML code that is used in a web page and that should indicate what the page is about. Each page of a website should ideally have a unique H1 tag. Here's what an H1 tag looks like in HTML code: <h1>Football Helmets</h1>.

EXHIBIT 6.4   Meta description tags from Ticketmaster.com and ESPN.com.

TICKETMASTER

```
<meta name="description" content="Find and buy tickets: concerts, sports, arts, theater, broadway shows, family events at Ticketmaster.com" />
```

ESPN

```
                            <meta name="description" CONTENT="ESPN.com provides comprehensive sports coverage.  Complete
sports information including NFL, MLB, NBA, College Football, College Basketball scores and news." />
                            <meta name="keywords" CONTENT="ESPN.com, ESPN, ESPN2, ESPNews, ESPN Classic, ESPNU, Insider,
sports scores, sports news, MLB scores, NFL scores, NBA scores, NHL scores, College Football scores, College Basketball
scores, sports videos, sports information, Fantasy sports, Fantasy games, Fantasy football, Fantasy baseball" />
```

Meta description tags.   This is a snippet of HTML code that includes a description of what a specific web page is about. This information is visible
as the text listed under the page's page title in SERPs, but it is not visible
to people who visit the website (Whalen, 2011). As with H1 tags and page
titles, each page on a website should have a unique meta description tag.
Most SEO professionals agree that meta descriptions do not carry much
weight in most search engine ranking algorithms, but they are still useful in helping a person see what the site is about when they are viewing
SERPs. A relevant and enticing description tag can help a page stand out
in the SERPs and gain additional clicks and traffic. See Exhibit 6.4 for an
example of the meta description from Ticketmaster.com and ESPN.com.

URL structure.   URL structure is an important on-site factor and one
that should be optimized for both users and search engines, to let them
know what the page is about and help them navigate the site.

The URLs for each page of a website should contain keywords that
are relevant to the content on the page. Ideally, no more than three to
five words should be used, and dashes should be placed between words
to separate them (Smarty, 2008). Look at the following URLs:

http://www.thisismywebsite.com/p?cat=153&prod=1489

http://www.thisismywebsite.com/s/product-name

The first URL has a poor structure compared with the second one, which
has been optimized. Exhibit 6.5 shows two examples of optimized URLs.

Other than page titles, none of the above elements will individually
make or break your SEO efforts. But there is no reason not to structure things properly. However, it's also important not to overthink the
words you choose. Google and other search engines look at whether or

EXHIBIT 6.5   Optimal URL structure.

PHOENIX SUNS SEASON TICKETS

Firefox ▾ | □ SUNS: Suns Season Tickets | **+**

← → □ http://www.**nba.com**/suns/season_tickets.html

ICEJERSEYS COLLEGE HOCKEY JERSEYS

Firefox ▾ | // NCAA College Hockey Jerseys, Caps, T-S... | **+**

← → // http://www.**icejerseys.com**/ncaa_college_hockey_jerseys.php

not pages have keywords that appear in a natural manner. Ultimately, sport organizations should focus on writing content that appeals to people instead of stuffing their pages with keywords.

Links

Links are perhaps the most important component of SEO. A link allows the user to jump directly from one web page to another web page. When bloggers link to a website, they believe the site will be valuable in some way. Search engines take this as a signal that the website is important (Krijestorac, 2010). Links are essentially the currency of search; the more links you have pointing to your site and specific pages, the better. For example, let's say two websites offer information about a gym in a certain city. Search engines consider the website that is linked to more often as having more authority than the site linked to less often. The website with greater authority will typically rank higher in SERPs.

Sport marketers should understand the three main link factors in SEO:

1. **Number of links.** As mentioned above, the more links to a website or page, the better.
2. **Quality of the links.** Links from high-quality websites (i.e., websites that have a high authority and a lot of links) are more valuable than links from lower quality websites.
3. **Anchor text to the specific page.** Anchor text is the actual text of a link that people can click on.

Search engines typically give anchor text a lot of weight in their algorithms because the linked text is usually relevant to the content on the page the link points to. Anchor text tells search engines what topic(s) the linked-to site has authority on. Ideally, companies want a link's anchor text to match or contain the keyword the linked page ranks for. Here are two anchor text examples:

- Buy MMA gloves
- Tim's MMA store

The anchor text in the first example is more beneficial to helping Tim's online store rank for the keyword phrase "buy MMA gloves," because it tells search engine algorithms what Tim's website is about.

Keywords, on-site elements, and links are the main components to SEO. Now let's move on to basic SEO strategy development.

SEO Strategy and Program Development

Developing an SEO strategy includes the following steps.

- Research
- Keyword analysis and selection
- Site analysis and optimization
- Link development
- Tracking/reporting

These steps are not meant to be a complete guide to SEO strategy, but they should help you understand the basic steps involved.

Research

An organization looking to use SEO should start by gathering information. They should conduct research on their industry, competitors, and products to see what people are searching for, what words their competitors rank for, and what opportunities exist to rank for specific keywords and phrases. This research should also focus on the company's current rankings in various search engines.

A variety of companies provide tools and software to help with SEO research, analysis, and management. A few examples include SEO Book, SEO Moz, My SEO Tool, and SEO Tool. If an organization wants to conduct some of this research on its own, it can use Google's free Keyword Tool (https://adwords.google.com) and type in search terms that describe its business. Google's Keyword Tool then presents a list of keyword ideas that show the number of searches monthly for keywords related to the organization's search terms and the level of

EXHIBIT 6.6   Google's Keyword Tool.

Google and the Google logo are registered trademarks of Google Inc., used with permission.

competition for each. The company can then search for these keywords in Google to see which of their competitors rank well in the search engines for them, and where opportunities might exist to rank for keywords that competitors aren't ranking for. Exhibit 6.6 includes an example of the information that Google's Keyword Tool provides for the search terms.

Keyword analysis and selection

In this phase, companies decide which keywords and key phrases they would like to focus their SEO efforts on. Keywords should be selected based on:

- Potential profitability and conversions (do they drive website visitors that are ready to complete a desired action?)
- Monthly search volume (are there enough people searching for this keyword to make it worth our efforts?)
- Difficulty factor (is this a keyword we can rank for, or are competitors too far ahead in terms of links and rankings?)

The number of keywords a company selects is usually based on the website's content, the level of competition for the terms being targeted, and how much work is required to optimize the site. For individual pages, a good rule is to target no more than three main keywords per page, because the page's content should be closely related to the keywords on which the company wants to focus.

Website analysis and optimization

Website analysis and optimization involves creating content that aligns with the target keywords and using the proper code (e.g., page titles and H1 tags) on each page. Additional pages or whole sections of the website may need to be developed to support the company's SEO efforts.

Link development

A link development strategy is a plan that enables a website to effectively gain links from other websites. Links can be gained three ways:

1. Manually inserting links in comments on other sites, forum posts, and online directories after providing a relevant comment. For example, a sport-related nonprofit may want to comment on blogs of other nonprofits and link back to its website to build up links.

2. Developing relationships with other website owners and bloggers and asking them to link to your website. For example, a shoe company could invite bloggers to an exclusive shoe release party in the hopes that these bloggers will write about the experience on their websites and link to the company's website.

3. Developing high-quality content that catches people's attention so that they want to link to your website. For example, a sport consulting company could release a free study that details the most popular retail brands in sport ranked by Twitter followers. This kind of study may catch people's attention so that they will want to write about it and link to it.

Ideally, a mix of these tactics works best for link development.

Tracking and reporting

Sport organizations should track their rankings for various keywords to see how increases and decreases in rankings for various keyword searches affect traffic and conversions. For example, before starting an SEO program, a local bowling center in Greensboro, North Carolina, may rank on the third results page for its main keyword "Greensboro bowling" and may only get five people per month requesting use of its lanes for birthday parties through its online form. The bowling center should track how its SEO efforts increase its ranking for "Greensboro bowling" and how this affects its website traffic and conversions each month.

The companies listed above in the research section offer tools that can be helpful in tracking SEO activities and results. Website analytics software—such as Google Analytics, Webtrends, and Omniture—can also be helpful in determining how SEO efforts are affecting key metrics, including website traffic, traffic sources, and conversions. Analytics will be discussed in Chapter 9.

SEO Challenges

SEO is a crucial component of a company's search marketing efforts. As you've seen, SEO includes many components and strategies that can affect an organization's ability to rank high in searches and drive relevant and profitable traffic to its website. However, as with any marketing tactic, SEO presents a few challenges for sport marketers.

Technical challenges

Part of SEO involves tweaking on-site elements and code to make websites more search-engine friendly. However, changing a website may require time, money, or resources an organization does not have. Sport organizations do not always have available technical skills on staff. In other cases, a team, league, or brand might sign an agreement with an outside company to create and control its website, leaving it in the hands of professionals. Depending on the agreement, changes and tweaks may simply not be possible, which can hinder overall success with SEO. When possible, it's important for sport marketers to build websites that can be easily updated.

Extended time for results

It can take months (or years) to see results from SEO efforts. As we've discussed, one of the most important factors in helping the search engines determine a website's relevance is the number and quality of links that point to the site. Getting these links and seeing meaningful changes in rankings (which lead to revenue increases) can take a long time. A company's competitors are likely generating new links and content as well, so it's often hard to say exactly how long an SEO program needs to operate before a company will start seeing results. Those that invest in SEO must be willing to be patient.

Search engine changes and updates

SEO is best viewed as an ongoing program to help generate more authority for a website and to increase its rankings in SERPs. However, certain elements are out of a sport marketer's control with SEO. Search engines are constantly updating their algorithms to produce more relevant results for their users. Factors that may have been important for SEO a year ago may no longer be as relevant today. Keeping up with such changes in search engines can be a challenge.

Competitor pressure

As more companies implement SEO programs, there is more competition for rankings in SERPs. Just because a company's website is at the top of the rankings doesn't mean it can afford to stop investing in SEO, since competitors are likely also trying to increase their own rankings.

Now that you have a solid understanding of the fundamentals of SEO, let's move on to paid search.

PAID SEARCH

While SEO involves on-site and off-site activities to help boost a website's rankings in the natural, or organic, search results (refer to Exhibit 6.1), paid search marketing enables companies to pay a fee to search engines (usually based on a cost-per-click) to show up in the sponsored listings on SERPs. As we mentioned earlier in the chapter, we won't be spending as much time on paid search, because it's not as tightly integrated with social media as SEO is. However, it is important for sport marketers to understand the basics and know what is possible.

Paid Search Overview

With paid search, companies pay search engines to display their ads in the sponsored results section of SERPs. The popular search engines have self-service, auction-based, advertising platforms that marketers can utilize to select which keywords they'd like their ads to show on SERPs and how much they're willing to spend for a click on their ad. This is known as the marketer's cost-per-click, or CPC. Paid search marketing is often referred to as pay-per-click marketing (PPC), even though PPC is a term that also can apply to ads that aren't based on search, such as the ad listings that appear on Facebook.

Google has remained the industry leader in paid search. According to the State of Search Marketing Report 2011 from the Search Engine Marketing Professional Organization, 95 percent of companies surveyed say they use Google's AdWords platform to place ads on Google search results pages. Seventy percent of respondents say they use the combined Yahoo! and Bing ad service (Enright, 2011).

Paid search has a few key benefits that sport marketers should consider. The main advantage is that it enables companies to quickly drive traffic to their websites. Instead of having to wait for website rankings to slowly rise in the organic search results through SEO, marketers can "pay to play" to have their ads appear in SERPs and quickly see an increase in traffic and conversions. This is also beneficial because companies only pay if someone clicks on the ad and visits the website, instead of paying per impression (a single instance of when an ad appears on a website), as is the case with CPM-based (cost per 1,000 impressions) advertising.

Another benefit of paid search campaigns is that they can be tested and improved quickly in certain situations. For example, a hockey team that is trying to sell tickets online may be seeing good results in clicks and conversions when its ad shows up for one keyword, but not another. Or maybe an ad with copy that reads "50% off tickets in July" is performing worse than an ad with copy that reads "Half off tickets in July." With paid search, sport marketers can quickly change ad headlines and copy so that the keyword ads appear in SERPs and adjust their budget to improve their campaign's performance.

Marketers can also target ads so they appear during certain times of the day or specify that only people in a certain location can see them. Search can target ads to groups of people based on certain criteria, such as time of day and the searcher's location (based on a user's IP address, which is a number assigned to each device that uses the

Internet). For example, a company that runs local basketball camps may only want its ads to appear to people who are in one of the cities near the camps.

The ability to tweak and test specific elements of paid search campaigns is a great advantage for sport marketers who are looking to refine their efforts and improve their overall ROI with paid search.

A final reason sport marketers should consider paid search in their online marketing efforts is that paid search and SEO often work hand in hand. Showing up for specific keyword searches in both the organic and paid listings of SERPs can help increase brand awareness, traffic, and sales. In one example, Omniture, an online retailer, ran an ad for a keyword search on its own brand name and occupied the first position in the natural listings. Appearing in the paid and organic listings for a search on its brand name led to a 24 percent increase in revenue per visit (Omniture, n.d.). Of course, this is just one example, but appearing in both the natural and paid listings is something that can impact a sport organization's results and should be tested accordingly. See Exhibit 6.7 for an example of how Dick's Sporting Goods appears in both the paid and organic listings in a Google search.

EXHIBIT 6.7   Dick's Sporting Goods in paid and natural search listings.

Key Components of Paid Search

Paid search has three key components:

1. Keyword-based bidding
2. Advertisements
3. Landing pages

Let's look at the basics of each of these components and why they are crucial to paid search success.

Keyword-based bidding

Popular search engines offer marketers self-service, auction-based advertising platforms that enable companies to bid on specific keywords that they would like their ads to show up for in SERPs. For example, a baseball team that is trying to sell tickets online—let's say the Atlanta Braves—may want their ads to show up when people search for phrases such as "Braves tickets," "Atlanta Braves tickets," and "Braves baseball tickets." Just as with SEO, keywords are crucial. The keywords that a company chooses to target should be relevant to what people are searching for and what content, goods, and/or services that the organization can offer.

As mentioned previously, keywords are purchased on a cost-per-click basis. The price of each keyword is determined by each search engine and is based on what other companies are paying for the same keyword. Most ad platforms enable companies to see what the cost-per-click will be for the top spot in the paid listings before they buy the ad. To gain the top placement for an ad, an organization simply has to outbid its competitors for a given keyword.

Advertisements

The second key component of paid search is the advertisement itself. In most cases, these are text-based ads that appear in the sponsored or paid sections of SERPs for specific keyword searches. Marketers can use the search engines' self-service advertising platforms to enter their own text and content to create these ads. For best results, it is important for ads to be relevant to a specific keyword search. For example, if a team (let's say the Durham Bulls) is looking to sell more jerseys online and target people searching for "Durham Bulls Jersey," it would be best for the team to run an ad that is relevant to this spe-

EXHIBIT 6.8   Components of paid search ad from Google's AdWords Beginners Guide (Google, n.d.).

Components of an ad

Here's how an AdWords text ad will look:

Advertise with Google
Want fast results?
Create your ad campaign today!
www.adwords.google.com

There are several elements that make up each ad:

- **Headline:** The first line of your ad acts as a link to your website. The best headlines relate directly to the keywords being searched, so try to include one of your keywords in your headline.

- **Lines of text:** Use these two lines to describe the product or service you're advertising. Since your ad space is limited, try to convey the key details and benefits of your product or service.

- **Display URL:** The last line (the text in green) is used to show the URL of the website you're promoting. The point of the display URL is to give users a clear idea of what website they'll be taken to when they click on the ad.

- **Destination URL:** You'll also set a destination URL which will not be visible in your ad. The destination URL (also called a landing page) is the exact page within your website which you want to send users directly to from your ad. Choose the page of your website that is most relevant to the product or service described in your ad.

Google and the Google logo are registered trademarks of Google Inc., used with permission.

cific search, instead of a generic ad that mentions all Durham Bulls merchandise.

Most paid search ads include four key elements: the headline, the lines of text, the display URL, and the destination URL. Exhibit 6.8 breaks down these components of a Google paid search ad, for example.

Remember that an ad's position in the sponsored listings depends on how much the company has bid for a specific keyword or set of keywords relative to its competitors. Other factors can come into play as well, such as the perceived quality of the ad, which is based on algorithms that determine how relevant the marketer's ad, keywords, and landing page are to people who see the ad.

The major paid search ad platforms also have built-in functionality for ad testing. Companies can design a variety of ads for a given campaign, which can be mapped to a keyword or group of keywords. Testing can be set up in the search engine so marketers can see which ads are performing better than others. Marketers can tweak the components of each ad and remove under-performing ads to maximize their ROI. Search marketing expert Dave Bilbrough provided the screenshot in Exhibit 6.9 that shows how data marketers can see from Google AdWords which ads perform best. Actual dollars have been blacked out to protect the client's privacy.

EXHIBIT 6.9 Data from Google AdWords ads.

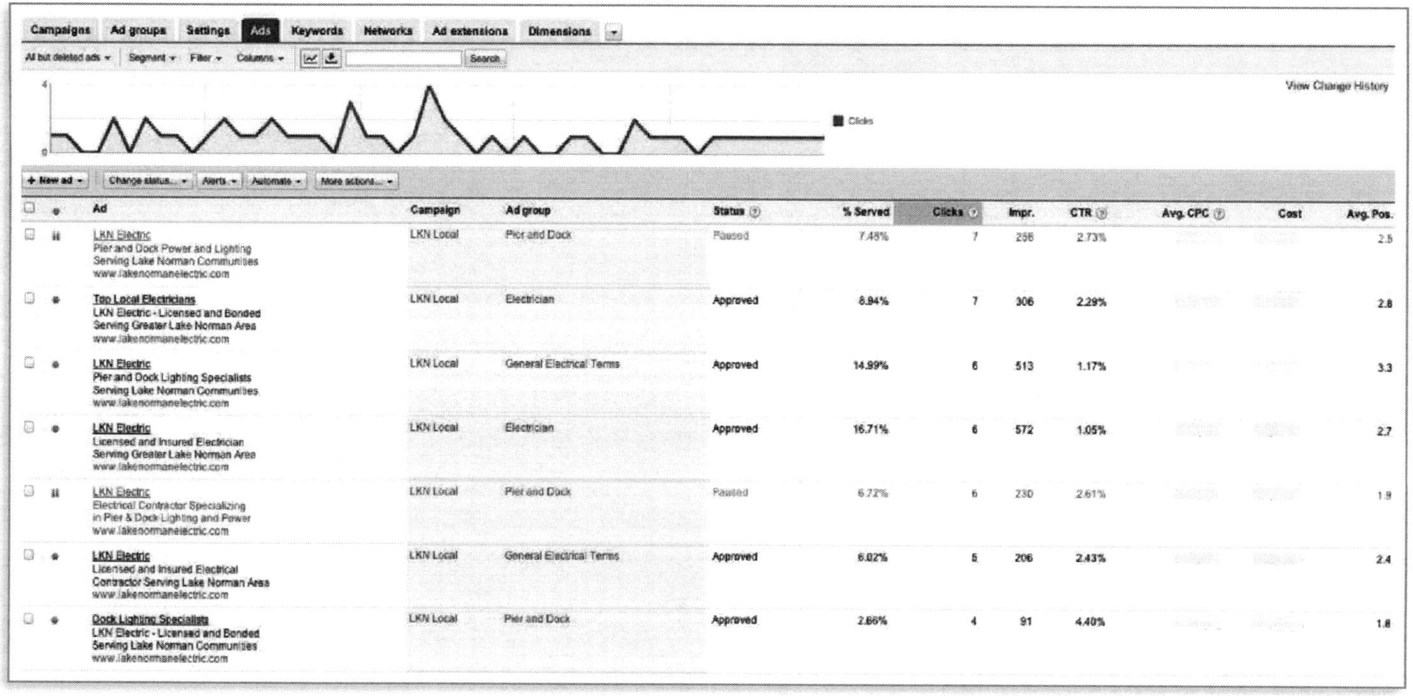

Google and the Google logo are registered trademarks of Google Inc., used with permission.

Landing pages

Landing pages are the third and final essential element of paid search campaigns. A landing page is the first web page someone sees after clicking on a company's page search ad. Landing pages don't always have to be an organization's home page. Instead, a good landing page should be the page that contains information about the specific product or service a person is searching for, as well as information on how the person can purchase the product/service or obtain more information about it. This information can be a mix of pictures, videos, and text-based content.

As with ads, landing pages should be relevant to the keyword for which a person is searching. They should make it easy for people to find more information about the topic of their search and to perform some action (e.g., purchase a product, make a donation, and so forth). For example, if an organization is advertising "basketball coaching software" and targeting this keyword search, the landing page should contain some images and copy relating to basketball coaching software, as well as the ability for people to see how they can purchase this software. This is much better than sending these people to a generic page about coaching software, since the page about basketball coaching software is more relevant to the search. If the page is not relevant to what the person is searching for, the person is more likely to leave the site and less likely to convert and complete the marketer's desired action.

Paid Search Strategy and Program Development

As with any new program, sport marketers should set goals when developing their paid search strategies and decide what actions they want people to take. For example, is the goal to sell tickets directly from the landing page? Or is the goal to get people to watch a video that explains why they should want to buy tickets?

Once the goals have been agreed upon, developing and managing a paid search campaign includes the following key steps:

- Research
- Campaign setup and design
- Tracking and ongoing management

Research

As with SEO, the first step in developing a paid search campaign is to conduct research on what a company's audience is searching for in order to see what opportunities exist to reach these people with ads in the paid listings on SERPs. It is also important to do some competitive research, to see the kind of ads an organization's competitors are running and the keywords they are targeting.

Sport marketers can take advantage of a variety of tools in researching and managing paid search campaigns. Some of these are free (e.g., Google AdWords Keyword Tool), while others will require an investment (e.g., Clickable, KeyCompete, and many others).

Campaign setup and design

In this phase of paid search, sport marketers should make sure their campaigns are properly set up. They should choose what search engines to advertise with and what keywords they'd like to target, based on monthly search volume, potential profitability, and keyword cost.

A variety of ads should be designed and mapped to the keywords (i.e., set up in the ad platforms so that the ad is relevant to the keyword) that have been selected, so that these ads can be tested and improved. One best practice is to include the keyword in the headline of the ad. The reason for this is simple. Whenever a user searches for a keyword and sees the resulting ad, the keyword phrase appears in bold font within the ad. This can help ads appear more noticeable to search engine users.

At the same time that ads are being designed, landing pages should be created or existing pages should be checked to make sure they are relevant to the ads and keywords that have been selected. Marketers should also experiment with testing various elements of landing pages to increase conversion rates and purchase amounts. For example, maybe having a red "Buy Now" button on a landing page will encourage more people to buy a certain product than having a blue "Buy Now" button. Or maybe adding video to text that explains the key features of a given product on the landing page will lead to more conversions. A variety of free tools (e.g., Google's Website Optimizer) as well as paid tools are available to help sport marketers test and optimize their landing pages.

Budgeting is also an important part of paid search campaigns. Search engine ad platforms typically enable marketers to set budgets that tell the search engines how many clicks the marketers are willing to pay for in a given day and/or month. After this budget is exhausted, the search engines no longer display the marketer's ad in the sponsored listings on SERPs. Careful budgeting is crucial to control spending and ensure that money is spent on the right keywords and ads to optimize the profitability of paid search campaigns.

Tracking and ongoing management

Like all marketing plans, paid search programs require ongoing tracking and management to be successful. Marketers must properly track campaigns so they can gauge their returns for specific keywords and ads. Revenue, conversion rates, and return on ad spending should be tracked for each keyword and ad.

Testing is also vital to success. Hundreds of elements can be tweaked and tested to improve traffic, conversions, and profitability. For example, a football team may find that more people click on paid search ads in the mornings, but more people buy tickets as a result of these clicks in the evenings. In this case, the team could experiment to see whether it should optimize its program so that its ads only appear at night, or if this would have a negative impact on its results.

Paid Search Challenges

Paid search offers many benefits to sport marketers, such as the ability to quickly drive targeted traffic to a specific webpage, track results, and test various elements to optimize conversions and overall spending. While paid search is definitely something that sport marketers should take advantage of, it also has a few challenges.

Competitive pressures

As more marketers invest in paid search, keyword costs will rise due to increased competition among advertisers. Rising cost-per-clicks mean that paid search costs are increasing, and this may make campaigns less profitable.

On an individual level, competitors can disrupt an organization's paid search program. For example, a keyword that was originally profitable for a marketer may suddenly become unprofitable if a competitor bids on it to drive up its cost-per-click. Many marketers must face this ongoing pressure from competitors.

Costs required to manage programs

As the name implies, paid ads cost money. Certain keywords—maybe even those that would be most effective—may prove to be expensive for marketers. Many elements of paid search campaigns can be monitored, tweaked, and tested so budgets are optimized, but this too can cost money. Like SEO, paid search campaigns require specialized knowledge. The time it takes to manage paid search campaigns and the costs associated with them can prove to be a challenge for sport marketers.

CONCLUSION

Sport marketers must consider search marketing part of their overall online marketing program. Search engines are still the most widely used channel in consumers' purchase decisions and can lead users to an organization's main website or even its social media channels. Combined with the proper approach to social media, search marketing can have a large impact on sport organizations' marketing efforts. As social media becomes more integrated with search, sport marketers must consider how search and social media can be integrated to increase awareness, traffic, and conversions.

REVIEW QUESTIONS

1. Why should sport marketers consider investing in search marketing programs?
2. Name two benefits of SEO and two benefits of paid search.
3. Why is it important for marketers to target the right keywords for SEO and paid search programs?
4. What are the key components of SEO? Of paid search?
5. Describe the steps a sport organization should take to develop an SEO program.
6. What are the key features of a paid search ad?
7. What do you think is most challenging about implementing an SEO program?
8. Create content for three paid search ads for your favorite sport organization that are geared at driving sales of a specific product or service. Explain your logic for the ad copy you create.

REFERENCES

Bing Team (2011, May 16). Facebook friends now fueling faster decisions on Bing. Retrieved from http://www.bing.com/community/site_blogs/b/search/archive/2011/05/16/news-announcement-may-17.aspx.

Doyle, J. (2010, March 16). New chart: How do your search conversion rates compare? Retrieved from http://www.marketingsherpa.com/article/how-do-your-search-conversion.

Enright, A. (2011, July 21). Companies are spending more on search, and outsourcing it more. Retrieved from http://www.internetretailer.com/2011/07/21/companies-are-spending-more-search-and-outsourcing-it-more.

Fishkin, R. (2011, June 22). Social annotations in search: Now your social network = rankings. Retrieved from http://www.seomoz.org/blog/social-annotations-in-search-now-your-social-network-rankings.

Google (n.d.). Adwords help. Retrieved from http://adwords.google.com/support/aw/bin/static.py?hl=en&topic=21903&guide=21899&page=guide.cs&answer=146296.

Han, Jin. (2011, June 16). May 2011 search market share report. Retrieved from http://blog.compete.com/2011/06/16/may-2011-search-market-share-report/.

Hare, P. (2009, July 27). H1 tag recommendations. Retrieved from http://www.submitawebsite.com/blog/2009/07/h1-tag-recommendations.html.

Krijestorac, H. (2010, August 10). Free eBook: Learning SEO from the experts. Retrieved from http://blog.hubspot.com/blog/tabid/6307/bid/6310/Free-eBook-Learning-SEO-From-The-Experts-A-Step-By-Step-Guide.aspx.

Omniture (n.d.). Buying your brand on search—up to 23% revenue lift! Retrieved from http://www.staging.omniture.com/en/resources/articles/marketing/buying_your_brand_on_search_up.

Performics (2010, September 30). Search engine usage study: How do your customers interact with search engines? Retrieved http://blog.performics.com/search/2010/09/search-engine-usage-study-how-do-your-customers-interact-with-search-engines.html.

Ramesh, P. (2011, February 11). New research: Search marketing vs. social media or search social media? Retrieved from http://www.livingstonbuzz.com/2011/02/28/new-research-search-marketing-vs-social-media-or-search-social-media/.

Smarty, A. (2008, July 3). SEO best practices for URL structure. Retrieved from http://www.searchenginejournal.com/seo-best-practices-for-url-structure/7216/.

Stelzner, M. (2011, April 7). 2011 social media marketing industry report. Retrieved from http://www.socialmediaexaminer.com/social-media-marketing-industry-report-2011/.

Website Marketing Services (n.d.). Search engine marketing definition. Retrieved from http://www.consultancymarketing.co.uk/search-engine-marketing-definition.htm.

Whalen, J. (2011, November 16). The meta description tag. Retrieved from http://www.highrankings.com/metadescription.

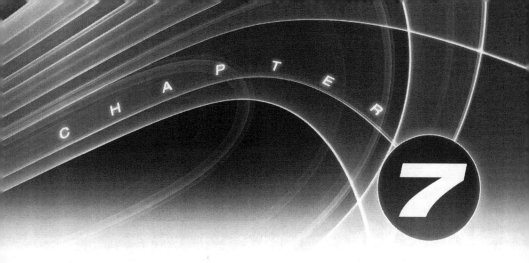

Mobile Marketing

INTRODUCTION

Let's move on to another important component of social media marketing—mobile marketing. According to the Mobile Marketing Association (n.d.), mobile marketing is a set of practices that enables organizations to communicate and engage with their audience in an interactive and relevant manner through any mobile device or network.

Sport marketers must know how to reach new customers through mobile marketing, as well as engage existing customers to create loyalty and new revenue streams through free and paid apps, ticket and merchandise sales, advertising, and sponsorship opportunities. In this chapter, we'll explore the rise of mobile devices and the various opportunities to reach people through these devices. We'll outline some best practices and give examples of how sport organizations are taking advantage of mobile devices and technologies to engage fans, unlock new sponsorship opportunities, and extend the reach of events and games. We'll also take a look at some challenges of mobile marketing.

ESPN

Everyone knows ESPN as the sport-centered cable television network with popular daily shows such as SportsCenter and live games. You probably have been to ESPN.com at some point to check scores, watch videos, or read news about your favorite team or athlete. Maybe you've also downloaded one of ESPN's apps to check scores on your favorite mobile device. In this study we explore how ESPN—despite some initial missteps—has strengthened its brand and extended its reach through a variety of mobile technologies and initiatives.

Since its launch in 1979, ESPN has expanded its coverage across many formats. The company produces more than 70,000 hours of programming annually over eight networks in the United States. More than 600 original pieces of content are created each day on ESPN.com (Ohlmeyer, 2011). Despite this success, the company's first foray into mobile was widely regarded as a flop. In November 2005, ESPN teamed with Sprint to launch Mobile ESPN, a cell phone service aimed at sports fans, complete with an ESPN-branded phone. In this venture, ESPN became a mobile virtual network operator (MVNO), which is a company that provides mobile phone services but does not have its own licensed frequency of the radio spectrum or its own infrastructure. As an MVNO, ESPN utilized Sprint's wireless network for service, sold its own handsets and subscription plans, and controlled marketing and billing. The phone's key feature was an application that enabled real-time updates on scores and provided news and highlights.

Despite investing $150 million into the service, the company reportedly only gained 30,000 subscribers before announcing that it would discontinue the business in September 2006 (ESPN's cell phone fumble, 2006). ESPN learned the hard way that it is tough to get people to switch plans; at the time, more than 70 percent of consumers had an existing plan (Belson, 2006).

After ESPN shut down its phone service, it began to have more success as a content provider. It relaunched ESPN Mobile by striking an exclusive deal with Verizon to make content available to subscribers of Verizon's V CAST service (Oswald, 2007). It has since partnered with other providers and expanded further into mobile marketing. For example, a deal with Sprint gave Sprint's mobile subscribers a pre-loaded content pack on select phones. Subscribers had access to ESPN news, scores, fantasy teams, and live programming (Kats, 2011).

Today, ESPN reaches its audience across many mobile devices and carriers through a variety of content and applications. On the iPhone alone, the company currently has 44 different apps available. See Exhibit 7.1 for a few examples categorized under ESPN's three main categories.

EXHIBIT 7.1 ESPN's mobile initiatives.

NEWS AND SCORES

ESPN Mobile Web: This delivers free access to ESPN news and scores. It's available on virtually all phones and carriers by visiting espn.mobi.

ESPN Alerts: These free alerts work on any device that can receive text messages and gives people access to scores, breaking news, and ESPN fantasy updates.

ESPN ScoreCenter: Available for iPhone, iPod Touch, the iPad, as well as Android devices, this free app enables people to get scores and updates from their favorite leagues and teams.

ESPN Radio App: The ESPN Radio App for iPhone, iPod Touch, and iPad ($4.99 in the iTunes App Store) enables fans to listen to select live Internet broadcasts from local ESPN affiliate stations, college football games broadcast on ESPN Radio, and select ESPN shows and podcasts.

VIDEO

ESPN Mobile TV: This app enables fans to watch select live events and ESPN programs on their mobile devices. It's available to Sprint, AT&T, and Verizon Wireless subscribers as well as on FLO TV devices.

ESPN Video On Demand: This service delivers daily clips and highlights from select games and TV shows. It's available to Verizon and Sprint customers as well as customers on other carriers through MobiTV.

WatchESPN: This enables fans to access live sports and shows from ESPN and is available on iPhone, iPod, iPad, and Android devices. Access is available to customers of Bright House Networks, Time Warner Cable, and Verizon FIOS TV as well as anyone with Verizon High Speed Internet (ESPN.com, n.d.).

GAMES AND TOOLS

ESPN Poker Club: Available to Verizon Wireless subscribers, this game lets players compete live against others from around the world.

ESPN Fantasy Football: This app ($1.99 in the iTunes App Store) enables fans to manage multiple fantasy football leagues and teams, make trades and lineup changes, and view scoring updates.

ESPN Passport: This free app utilizes GPS technology that is built into Apple products to enable fans to "check in" to games they're attending, share comments on games and photos with other fans, and keep track of games they've attended previously.

(continued)

ESPN's mobile initiatives have enabled it to reach sports fans through a variety of content and created new revenue streams. Its success earned the company the "Mobile Publisher of the Year" award from eMarketer in 2010; as Kristy Young, director of product development at ESPN said, their mobile initiative "allows us to be present wherever, whenever sports are watched, listened to, discussed, debated, read about or played" (Tsirulnik, 2010).

At the end of 2010, ESPN was the leading mobile web sports site and the eighth most-trafficked site on the mobile web overall. Almost 3.5 billion ESPN Mobile alerts were delivered to fans in 2010, up nearly 300 percent from the year before. Nearly 10 million sports fans have downloaded the ESPN ScoreCenter application, and 95 percent have personalized their user experience by tracking their favorite leagues and teams (Tsirulnik, 2010).

ESPN continues to dominate the sports media landscape due to its ability to engage fans in unique ways across multiple platforms. In order for ESPN to maintain its mobile marketing position in the future, it must continue to innovate.

THE RISE OF MOBILE MARKETING IN SPORTS

We offered one definition of mobile marketing at the beginning of the chapter. Another definition comes from mobile marketing expert Matti Leppäniemi, who defines it as "using interactive wireless media to provide customers with time and location sensitive, personalized information that promotes goods, services and ideas, thereby generating value for all stakeholders" (2008).

There are now more ways than ever to engage fans with content and experiences through their mobile devices. You can reach fans through mobile devices at a sporting event, while they're home watching a sporting event, when they're looking for information about a sporting event (or team, player, coach, etc.), or searching for some other sports content or experience.

Mobile marketing has become important, and this importance will only increase in the future. The single greatest factor contributing to the rise of mobile marketing is the increased use of cell phones. At the end of 2011, the number of mobile subscribers worldwide was estimated to have surpassed 6 billion (International Telecommunication Union, 2011). CTIA, the wireless communications trade association, estimates that there are about 332 million mobile subscribers in the United States (CTIA, 2011). That's roughly equivalent to 104 percent of the U.S. population; some people have more than one device and subscribe to multiple service providers.

Mobile data and Internet usage also continue to increase. Consider the popularity of text messaging. Three-quarters of all U.S. adult cell phone owners send and receive text messages. Cell phone users between the ages of 18 and 24 exchange an average of 3,200 texts per month (Smith, 2011). More than half of all adult cell phone owners also use their phones to browse the Internet, and 17 percent of them do most of their online browsing on their phone (Smith, 2012).

As mobile penetration and usage increase, the number of consumers who own smartphones has also increased. Smartphones are mobile phones with built-in operating systems, applications, and Internet access compared with feature phones, which are typically less expensive and offer less functionality. By the end of 2011, smartphones were outselling desktop personal computers (Arthur, 2011).

As mobile penetration has increased, wireless providers and handset manufacturers are striking deals with U.S. sport organizations. For example, in March 2010, Verizon signed a $720 million, four-year partnership with the NFL to be the league's official wireless partner. The NBA and the NHL also have official wireless partners, T-Mobile and Verizon respectively. These partnerships can be a great revenue stream for leagues, and they provide new content opportunities for fans.

Selling tickets to live events via mobile devices is an important area for sport marketers. Consider this: According to Juniper Research, about two billion tickets for sports and other events were purchased via mobile devices in 2009, and this number is projected to rise to 15 billion by 2014 (Perez, 2010). Mobile tickets are a win for fans and marketers alike; fans gain the convenience of having their tickets easily accessible on their mobile devices and marketers save money by not having to print paper tickets. However, paperless tickets do not have the collector value that some fans crave.

Perhaps the most important reason sport marketers need to consider mobile marketing is because mobile devices are always available. Unlike live events, where people must set aside time and be in a certain place to view it, mobile content can be consumed almost anywhere. The Internet was the first major technology that enabled individuals to find sports content and marketers to reach fans at any time. In addition, the always-on nature of mobile devices integrates well with social media, which is all about people connecting and communicating, often in real-time. Sports fans can be engaged at the stadium through mobile device applications and browsers, which can be used to promote coupons, sweepstakes, games, and other information. For example, in September 2011, the Purdue Boilermakers women's volleyball team hosted a "Social Media Night" during their match against Michigan State. As part of the event, fans were encouraged to post photos of themselves in school colors and participate in contests on Twitter (PurdueSports.com, 2011).

Fans who are not able to attend games can have sports experiences and content delivered to them in other ways. A recent study by Yahoo! found that 86 percent of people with access to mobile Internet used their mobile device while watching TV (Hogg, 2011). This has unlocked new opportunities for sport marketers to reach fans, which we'll explore in the next section.

MOBILE MARKETING TACTICS, EXAMPLES, AND BEST PRACTICES

 arketers can take advantage of mobile tactics and campaigns to reach fans in many ways.

SMS/Text Messaging

Text messaging is the most popular activity among mobile users. Many teams and sports brands utilize SMS (short message service) campaigns to send news, scores, coupons, and other updates to mobile phone users and enable them to enter contests and sweepstakes. For example, a local sports retail store might enable its customers to receive text messages about last minute sales. A nonprofit could create a program that would allow people to text the word "volunteer" to a phone number to initiate their involvement in a specific effort.

Most teams and leagues have mobile subscriber programs, as do many other sport organizations. In 2010, the NBA's Cleveland Cavaliers were already sending their mobile subscribers more than 1.5 million text messages per month regarding statistics, scores, news, and other updates (Olson, 2010). Many sport marketers have built their programs so that subscribers can pick and choose what kind of updates to receive.

Fans can opt-in to receive text messages by filling out an online form so the marketer has access to the fan's phone number. Marketers can also register a branded short code—a five- or six-digit number—that fans can send a text message to in order to opt-in to receiving text messages or engage with the marketer. Most programs are set up so that fans can text the word "stop" to the code at any time to opt-out of receiving messages, as shown in Exhibit 7.2.

Some teams, such as the NBA's Dallas Mavericks, have gone further and have enabled fans to interact with the team (and with other fans) in the arena and during game broadcasts via text messaging (Dallas Mavericks, 2011). For example, the team shows live polls during games and fans can participate by texting their answer. Answers are compiled and calculated on-screen, using technology from the Mavericks' partner, Txtstation Mobile Marketing.

Another example of an SMS campaign is giving people the ability to text a short code in order to enter a contest or sweepstakes. A sponsor

EXHIBIT 7.2 Opt-in form for NBA text alerts.

Siource: Courtesy of NBA.

Columbus Blue Jackets Text2Win promotion

As an official partner of the NHL Columbus Blue Jackets, Nationwide created the Text2Win campaign as part of its activation during the 2009–2010 season.

For Text2Win, fans texted "nationwide" to win an autographed Blue Jackets jersey during each home game. The Text2Win entry time for each game began about one hour before faceoff and ended at the start of the third period. The winning fan received a text that he or she won and should claim the prize at the customer services desk. The response rate was reasonably high for this type of promotion; on average, 9 percent of fans in attendance entered the Text2Win each game. Messaging in the arena promoting the Text2Win included signage, PA announcements, video board prompts, signs held by the Pepsi Power Patrol (the Blue Jackets cheerleaders), and a promotional video featuring Stinger the mascot and the Power Patrol.

Nationwide was so pleased with the response rate and success of the Text2Win that they decided to do it again for the 2010–2011 season with slight changes in the prizes.

could promote a weekly All-Star game ticket giveaway to anyone who opts-in to receiving mobile alerts during that time. This is often a low-cost and effective way to drive leads.

As you've seen, SMS text messaging campaigns can stand alone or they can be integrated with other types of media. Here are a few best practices for SMS campaigns:

- **Require opt-ins.** Always ensure that people have opted-in to receive content from you before sending them anything. Also, make sure people know how often they'll be receiving messages from you and understand they can opt-out at any time.

- **Keep it simple.** Text messages are simple by nature. Each update you send should have a single message or unique call to action. Adding multiple calls-to-action can be confusing, and sending too many messages can irk subscribers.

- **Provide a clear benefit.** Think about why a fan would want to receive messages from you via their mobile device. Consider offering an incentive, such as exclusive content or coupons, to reward people for signing up.

Mobile Websites

Use of mobile apps is growing, but a majority of mobile users and sports fans still use their mobile browsers more than apps. In 2010, 67 percent of U.S. mobile users preferred to access sports feeds, scores, news stories and fantasy leagues through their mobile browsers (eMarketer, 2010), though use of apps has of course increased since then. Users also prefer to use browsers to research specific product and price information, register online for offers and promotions, receive online promotions, purchase products, and share information with friends.

IDATE (2011) predicted that, worldwide, in 2013 there would be more mobile Internet users worldwide than fixed Internet users, and that by 2015, there will be more than 2.3 billion mobile Internet users. Sport marketers must not overlook the importance of having a mobile version of their website. See Exhibit 7.3 for an example of the non-mobile and mobile versions of NikeLab.com.

Best practices for mobile website design include (Chapman, 2010):

- Simple layouts
- Scrolling in one direction
- No pop-up banners
- Avoiding Javascript and other elements that are not supported by mobile devices
- Giving users the option to visit the standard site instead

EXHIBIT 7.3   NikeLab.com: PC version (left) and mobile version (right).

Source: Courtesy of NikeLab.com

Mobile Advertising

Mobile advertising encompasses a variety of formats and opportunities. Some mobile display ads are placed through third-party ad networks that place them in applications and websites for mobile devices, banner advertising on select mobile sites, paid search advertising, games and applications, and mobile video ads. These ads can direct consumers to mobile websites, games, ticket offers, and can drive awareness and leads or mention specific offers and discounts.

Mobile advertising spending in the United States was estimated to reach $2.3 billion in 2012, up 97 percent over 2011 (eMarketer, 2012). Adopting a mobile advertising strategy will be an increasingly important part of sport marketer's overall digital advertising efforts. Also, creating new advertising and sponsorship opportunities for brands can help organizations drive additional revenue from their mobile content and initiatives.

Sport marketers can take advantage of mobile advertising to target fans according to a variety of criteria:

- **Location:** Marketers can find users through GPS or wireless tower signals, check-ins at local businesses through social apps, and by using ZIP codes or areas entered in search or weather queries. For example, a team could partner with a local restaurant to offer a ticket discount to anyone who checks in to the restaurant on Foursquare, a location-based social networking website.

- **Wireless provider:** Marketers can target customers from a given wireless provider, such as Verizon or AT&T.

- **Handset/Operating system:** Marketers can target users of various mobile phones and operating systems. For example, a marketer could partner with a manufacturer to have its ads appear within a game that comes preloaded on a certain phone.

- **Demographics:** Marketers can often target users in a specific gender, age range, and other data. For example, a women's soccer league could build brand awareness by working with a mobile ad network to target women from ages 18 to 34.

- **Contextual:** Marketers can run ads based on content on a mobile website. For example, a marketer could partner with a news website to advertise within its sports section.

One brand to take advantage of mobile advertising on a sports-related mobile site was Chevrolet. In 2010, the auto company struck a deal with

ESPN for exclusive sponsorship of ESPN's College Bowl Mania portal and game. This game enabled college football fans to pick winners of each bowl game. Fans could access the game via ESPN Mobile Web or an iPhone or Android app (Butcher, 2010a). This sponsorship was an interesting way for Chevrolet to advertise its new Cruze sedan to ESPN's fans.

There are a few models in place for purchasing or selling mobile advertising. Typically, these ads are purchased on a cost-per-click basis or cost-per-thousand impressions, though other metrics are sometimes used, such as a cost-per-download or lead (e.g., someone who opted-in to receive information by submitting his or her email address). However, mobile advertising formats and options are constantly evolving, and sport marketers must keep up with these changes to take advantage of additional opportunities as they arise.

Mobile Apps

Mobile apps are software programs that run on smartphones, tablets, and other mobile devices and provide users with direct access to various types of content, including text, pictures, videos, music, and games. The apps bypass the need for people to use a web browser and may be free or paid. They may exist on their own or as extensions of a brand's website or other content initiatives.

The increasing market penetration of smartphones means that use of mobile apps is also increasing. For sport marketers, there are three major players in the app world to keep an eye on: RIM (Blackberry), Apple, and Android. Each of these has a different operating system, so an app written for a device using one operating system will not run on a device using another operating system. According to data from Kantar World-Panel ComTech, Android is the most popular in the United States, with 57.5 percent of the market share. Apple came in second place, with 35.7 percent, followed by RIM with 2.1 percent (Kantar WorldPanel, 2012).

Apps are usually downloaded from the operating systems' mobile app stores. Technology research firm Gartner Research estimated that app stores worldwide attracted 17.7 billion downloads in 2011, a 117 percent increase over 2010. While Android may lead the smartphone market, Apple is the clear leader in terms of number of apps downloaded. An estimated nine out of every 10 app downloads in 2010 came from Apple's App Store, according to research by Gartner, for a total of over 10 billion app downloads (Buelva, 2011).

Sport marketers can get involved with mobile applications in two ways: building their own branded applications or engaging with users of an existing mobile application through content creation, sponsor-ship, and advertising options.

Branded applications

Building an application is one way to engage fans through mobile de-vices. All of the major U.S. professional sports leagues have their own mobile applications and many pro teams do as well.

Branded apps from leagues and teams typically give fans the abil-ity to check schedules and scores and view game statistics and recaps. Other features may include the ability to check in to games, the ability to predict game winners, the ability to chat with other fans, and access to premium video content. For example, the NBA Game Time app is available for several smartphone platforms. Fans have access to scores, stats, and schedules and the ability to check in to games in person or on TV. Users share their picks with other fans using the app and with friends on social networks such as Twitter and Facebook. Fans earn points for checking in and compete against other users to unlock virtu-al badges, NBA prizes, and special discounts. An app upgrade for $9.99 allows fans to bypass all advertisements and access video highlights, home and away radio feeds, team-produced video, and push notifica-tions. Users can also opt to pay $39.99 for the NBA League Pass mobile app, which allows the user to watch up to 40 games per week live.

The NBA is one of many sport organizations that creates its own apps. Athletes, coaches, colleges, fitness centers, and sports-centric retail brands are creating apps to engage fans in new ways. NFL wide receiver Chad Johnson, for example, has an iPhone app that gives fans access to his latest Twitter updates, his game schedule, videos, photos, game statistics, and audio clips. Fans can also ask Johnson questions direct-ly through the app. Athletes and coaches who have their own apps can reach their biggest fans and provide more behind-the-scenes updates and content than can be found on many team and media websites. This helps build fan loyalty. Sport marketers may want to build their own apps to give fans a rich media experience that includes pictures and videos, allow them to access content when they do not have an Internet connection, and let them take advantage of a phone's built-in features, such as GPS.

Some important things to consider when thinking of building a branded app include:

- Budget restraints
- Type of mobile operating system used most by the target audience

- Type of content and experiences that will be delivered
- Resources needed for future updates
- Purchase price

Engaging fans through existing mobile applications

Sport marketers should also consider which apps their target audience may already be using and how they can engage fans through them.

Remember that the most popular applications are often related to social media or gaming. Consider that Facebook, the world's largest social network, had more than 540 million people using Facebook apps in June 2012 (Facebook, n.d.) and Twitter has apps for Android, iPhone, and RIM devices. Mobile phones are a perfect fit for social media outreach and engagement, because they enable consumers to easily receive information and content in real time. So it's important to think about how sport marketers can reach people who are already using these apps. Why not ask people to answer select questions on these networks, post the answers on the organization's Facebook page, and reward the best ones? What about asking fans to share pictures and videos from pre-game tailgating as part of a promotion?

Beyond social networking, a growing category of apps that can be used to engage sport fans is location-based services. These applications utilize GPS functionality that is built into some mobile devices to enable people to check in at various locations and tell friends what they're doing. Examples of location-based services include Foursquare and Facebook Places.

Check-ins from location-based services are often linked with Facebook and/or Twitter. This is important because businesses can gain additional exposure when people check in and their friends see these check-ins. One way sport organizations can encourage more check-ins (and thus gain more exposure) is by offering virtual and real-world rewards and discounts for them. The box on p. 148 considers how one team did this.

Despite the Redskins success with this promotion, keep in mind that location-based services are still in their infancy. For comparison sake, Foursquare reportedly has over 20 million users (Foursquare, 2012); Facebook has over 955 million (Facebook, n.d.). On any given day, only 1 percent of U.S. adults use a service that enables them to share their location, according to a report by the Pew Research Center's Internet & American Life Project (Zickuhr, 2010). These apps are interesting, but they may need to give users more than just the ability to check in and gain virtual badges in order to become more popular.

Redskins Reward Loyal Fans for Foursquare Check-ins

As an experiment during the 2010 football season, the NFL Washington Redskins utilized Foursquare to reward fans for checking in at FedEx Field during games and at select bars across Washington, DC. The team became the first NFL team with its own virtual badge, a graphic symbol that appears on the profile pages of Foursquare users, which fans could unlock after checking in at the team's stadium or at one of nearly 30 bars in the area.

Having a badge is nice, but the Redskins knew that rewarding fans with real-world experiences and incentives would entice more people to check in. Fans who unlocked the Redskins badge were automatically entered into a sweepstakes to win two tickets to a game against the Philadelphia Eagles. The Redskins also incorporated a sponsor, GEICO, into the promotion. In addition to the tickets, the winner also received the chance to tailgate with the GEICO caveman before the game.

The Redskins advertised their Foursquare promotion at preseason games on the Jumbotron and with preseason TV advertising. The team also promoted the initiative through email and on the team's website.

According to Shripal Shah, senior vice president and chief strategy officer at the Washington Redskins, "the contest exceeded our expectations." Ultimately, the promotion resulted in over 20,000 check-ins at FedEx Field during the team's seven home games in 2010 and over 30,000 check-ins at participating bars (Hibbard, 2010).

There are also privacy implications with location-based services. According to a report by Microsoft, more than half of users are concerned about the potential loss of privacy by publicly checking in at places (Rubin, 2010). Sport marketers should keep an eye on this growth area but tread carefully.

Advertising within mobile apps

Many mobile apps, especially free ones, are supported by advertising and can be used by sport marketers to target fans. For example, a marketer could work with a game app and have its ad appear each time users make a certain move in the game. Two important factors to consider when creating a mobile advertising campaign are ensuring that the ads are relevant to fans and that they don't disrupt fans' mobile usage. Findings from a survey of mobile users conducted by Harris Interactive found that 71 percent of respondents indicated a preference for ads that allowed them to remain in the app they were using. A majority of respondents (63 percent) also expressed a preference for ads that allow them to sign up for coupons, deals, or newsletters (Pontiflex, 2010).

Mobile Commerce

According to the Mobile Marketing Association, mobile commerce is the one- or two-way trade for something of value achieved by a mobile electronic device. Mobile commerce is a growing trend; in 2010, one in five U.S. adult consumers reported having made a purchase in the past month (Mobile Marketing Association, 2010). Among smartphone owners, at least 41 percent had made a purchase via their phone (Siwicki, 2011). The most common mobile commerce activity is purchasing device content (e.g., ring tones and apps). The second most popular activity is a tie between using discounts and coupons and purchasing physical goods or non-mobile content and services. Purchasing tickets to events or for travel was the third most popular mobile commerce activity (Mobile Marketing Association, 2010).

Consumers use their mobile devices for shopping in two ways—researching and making actual purchases. While this trend is still growing, sport marketers should take this information into account when designing mobile websites and apps. If mobile shopping continues to rise, fans will soon expect to be able to purchase tickets and merchandise directly from their phones. At games, they may even use their mobile device to look up information on concessions, so start thinking about how your organization can build such functionalities into its apps and mobile websites to enhance fans' experiences at games.

Mobile coupons are another concept to watch. In addition to giving fans the ability to receive coupons via SMS messages, consider giving them access to select deals and discounts through your organization's mobile website.

Sponsors and advertisers can also tap into apps and mobile websites to offer fans coupons. The launch of the mobile app for Sports Radio 810 WHB was sponsored by a group of Kansas City Goodyear dealers (Butcher, 2010b). When the app launched in September 2010, the Goodyear Platinum Independent Tire Dealers offered a free oil change to the first 100 people who clicked on the coupon in the app's deals section. All 100 coupons were claimed by 1:00 pm on the day the app launched.

Mobile commerce, including shopping and coupons, is a critical feature in sport marketers' mobile marketing strategies.

MOBILE MARKETING STRATEGY

 good mobile marketing strategy consists of:

- Understanding how the target audience uses their mobile devices and what kind of content they are interested in.
- Developing a goal-based program.
- Selecting content and assets that engage fans.
- Determining the best ways to reach fans on mobile devices.

Understanding the Audience

Researching the type of content the sport marketer's target audience is looking for (and what formats they prefer) is the first step in creating a mobile strategy. Also conduct research to find out what mobile devices and operating systems fans are using. You should never just decide the company needs a certain type of application without first making sure that enough fans would utilize it.

Developing a Goal-Based Program

An organization may be looking to drive traffic to a website, Facebook page, or Twitter feed; sell more tickets and merchandise; get fans to engage with sponsors; gain feedback; or obtain some other goal. Carefully consider the organization's goals when developing a mobile strategy. For example, a strategy that is geared toward selling more tickets will be significantly different from a strategy that is focused on changing fan perceptions. Also consider how a mobile program will fit with the organization's overall marketing goals and objectives. Lastly, consider budgets and resources, which will affect what can and cannot be accomplished.

Selecting Content and Assets

Sport marketers should examine current assets to see how they can be leveraged for a mobile campaign. Organizations looking to partner with sponsors and advertisers on their mobile efforts should also look at what assets and resources their partners and sponsors have (or what they would want). Is the behind-the-scenes or exclusive content that fans want access to available? Do you need to dedicate resources to creating new content and experiences that will engage fans through mobile devices? What kind of resources will be used to promote the mobile campaign? All of these questions must be addressed.

Choosing the Best Ways to Reach Fans

As we've discussed, sport marketers can take advantage of a variety of tactics and opportunities in the mobile marketplace. Choosing the right platforms and mix of tactics is an important part of an organization's mobile marketing plan. You must understand the various mobile devices and operating systems fans use, as well as how they use their mobile devices, in order to select the appropriate platforms and tactics for your organization. One way to do this is to survey fans or work with an agency that specializes in mobile marketing.

MOBILE MARKETING CHALLENGES

Mobile marketing is growing as smartphone market penetration increases and opportunities to reach fans in new ways continue to proliferate. Despite this, sport marketers face several challenges.

Difficult to Integrate

When the Internet first arrived, many companies created digital business divisions and treated their web businesses separately from their overall business. This created many problems, including a lack of a consistent brand experience for customers and a lack of integration between the company's offline and online businesses.

These same problems may affect organizations that lack a clear mobile marketing strategy or have one that is not adequately integrated into their overall business objectives. As more people become comfortable using their mobile devices for information, communication, and product purchases, marketers must ensure that their initiatives provide an outstanding user experience and that they don't treat their mobile marketing programs like many companies treated their initial e-commerce programs.

Lack of Best Practices and Research

As with any growing industry, it's often hard to find best practices and research to guide, plan, and execute successful campaigns. Experimentation can be good, but it can also be costly if it is not a success.

Mobile Apps vs. Mobile Websites Debate

Many people debate whether sport marketers should build mobile apps or mobile websites. In our view, this debate is irrelevant. Mobile websites *and* mobile apps need to be considered when designing your mobile marketing strategy.

Complicated Relationships Between Content Providers and Carriers

Issues regarding exclusivity and access to content will arise when content providers, such as leagues and teams, strike exclusive relationships with carriers and mobile device manufacturers. Fans may have a hard time understanding why they don't have access to the same content their friends have, simply because they don't have the same wireless provider. You must communicate new deals clearly to fans to avoid confusion and anger.

Consumer Confusion over Advertising and Sponsorship

The mobile industry is still relatively new, so many consumers are just now interacting with mobile content. Marketers are also experimenting with advertising and sponsorship formats that integrate into applications and aren't too disruptive for consumers. It takes time for people to get used to new features and functionality and to differentiate between advertising and content. Unfortunately, about 47 percent of mobile app users say they tap on mobile ads more often by mistake than they do on purpose, according to a survey by Harris Interactive (Claburn, 2011). This may mean that advertising formats are confusing to consumers and that a large percentage of mobile advertising budgets are being wasted.

CONCLUSION

The rise in mobile phone usage and the always-on nature of mobile devices are two of the most important reasons why sport marketers should embrace mobile marketing. Many social media platforms and websites also have mobile components that marketers should be aware of. Despite being relatively new, mobile marketing is an important aspect of any successful sport marketer's multichannel marketing program.

REVIEW QUESTIONS

1. What forces are shaping the rise of mobile marketing?
2. What are some best practices for text messaging campaigns?
3. What are some of the key features in mobile apps for sports leagues and teams?
4. What are the four main steps in creating a mobile marketing strategy? What factors should organizations consider at each step?
5. What do you think is the biggest challenge facing sport organizations in mobile marketing?

REFERENCES

Arthur, C. (2011, June 5). How the smartphone is killing the PC. *Guardian.* Retrieved from http://www.guardian.co.uk/technology/2011/jun/05/smartphones-killing-pc.

Belson, K. (2006, September 28). Mobile ESPN to end service aimed at sports customers. *New York Times.* Retrieved from http://www.nytimes.com/2006/09/29/technology/29phone.html.

Buelva, A. (2011, January 29). Revenues of global mobile app stores to exceed $15 B. Retrieved from http://208.184.76.180/business/telecoms/652320/revenues-of-global-mobile-app-stores-to-exceed-15-b.

Butcher, D. (2010a, December 21). Chevrolet drives Cruze awareness via ESPN mobile web sponsorship. Retrieved from http://www.mobilemarketer.com/cms/news/advertising/8542.html.

Butcher, D. (2010b, September 21). Goodyear distributes mobile coupons via local sports radio app. Retrieved from http://www.mobilecommercedaily.com/2010/09/21/goodyear-distributes-mobile-coupons-via-local-sports-radio-app.

Chapman, C. (2010, February 9). Mobile web design: Tips and best practices. Retrieved from http://www.noupe.com/how-tos/mobile-web-design-tips-and-best-practices.html.

Claburn, T. (2011, January 28). Half of mobile ads clicked by mistake. Retrieved from http://www.informationweek.com/news/software/bi/showArticle.jhtml?articleID=229200047&cid=RSSfeed_IWK_All.

CTIA (2011, December). Wireless quick facts. Retrieved from http://www.ctia.org/advocacy/research/index.cfm/AID/10323.

Dallas Mavericks shoot and score with Txtstation partnership (2011, January 17). Retrieved from http://www.mobilemarketingwatch.com/dallas-mavericks-shoot-and-score-with-txtstation-partnership-12603/.

eMarketer (2010, October 27). Mobile users prefer browsers over apps. Retrieved from http://www.emarketer.com/Article.aspx?R=1008010.

eMarketer (2012, August 1). US to top Japan as world's biggest mobile ad market. Retrieved from http://www.emarketer.com/PressRelease.aspx?R=1009228.

ESPN's cell-phone fumble (2006, October 29). *Bloomberg Businessweek Magazine*. Retrieved from http://www.businessweek.com/magazine/content/06_44/b4007026.htm.

ESPN.com (n.d.). What is WatchESPN? Retrieved from http://espn.go.com/espn3/mobile.

Facebook (n.d.). Key facts. Retrieved from http://newsroom.fb.com/content/default.aspx?NewsAreaId=22.

Foursquare (2012, April). About foursquare. Retrieved from https://foursquare.com/about/.

GPS Business News (n.d.). Nielsen: US smartphone penetration to be over 50 in 2011. Retrieved from http://www.gpsbusinessnews.com/Nielsen-US-Smartphone-Penetration-to-Be-over-50-in-2011_a2154.html.

Hibbard, C. (2010, December 28). Washington Redskins kick-off Foursquare to reward loyal fans. Retrieved from http://www.socialmediaexaminer.com/washington-redskins-kick-off-foursquare-to-reward-loyal-fans/.

Hogg, C. (2011, January 26). Study: 86% of people use mobile devices while watching TV. Retrieved from http://digitaljournal.com/article/302941.

IDATE (2011, September 16). Mobile internet users will overtake fixed users in 2013. Retrieved from http://blog.idate.fr/?p=911.

International Telecommunication Union (2011). The world in 2011: ICT facts and figures. Retrieved from http://www.itu.int/ITU-D/ict/facts/2011/material/ICTFactsFigures2011.pdf.

Kantar WorldPanel (2012, October 30). OS (operating system) share - smartphone sales. Retrieved from http://www.kantarworldpanel.com/dwl.php?sn=news_downloads&id=85.

Kats, R. (2011, January 5). ESPN offers packaged mobile content deal to sprint subscribers. Retrieved from http://www.mobilemarketer.com/cms/news/content/8675.html.

Leppäniemi, M. (2008, June 7). Mobile marketing communications in consumer markets. Department meeting of the Faculty of Economics and Business Administration at the University of Oulu, Finland.

Mobile Marketing Association (n.d.). MMA updates definition of mobile marketing. Retrieved from http://mmaglobal.com/news/mma-updates-definition-mobile-marketing.

Mobile Marketing Association (2010, May 19). One in five U.S. adult consumers now using mobile commerce. Retrieved from http://www.mmaglobal.com/news/one-five-us-adult-consumers-now-using-mobile-commerce.

NBA game time (n.d.). Retrieved from http://www.nba.com/mobile/gametime/.

Ohlmeyer, D. (2011, January 26). Can you hear me now? Retrieved from http://sports.espn.go.com/espn/columns/story?columnist=ohlmeyer_don&id=6063051.

Olson, E. (2010, September 20). Bonding with fans who can't get enough. *New York Times*. Retrieved from http://www.nytimes.com/2010/09/21/business/media/21adco.html.

Oswald, E. (2007, February 8). Mobile ESPN makes its return on Verizon. Retrieved from http://www.betanews.com/article/Mobile-ESPN-Makes-its-Return-on-Verizon/1170948387.

Perez, S. (2010, February 2). Mobile ticketing taking off: 15 billion sold by 2014. Retrieved from http://www.readwriteweb.com/archives/mobile_ticketing_taking_off_15_billion_sold_by_2010.php.

Pontiflex (2010, December). December 2010 Harris interactive survey: how consumers interact with mobile app advertising. Retrieved from http://www.pontiflex.com/media/2012/04/HowConsumersInteractwithMobileAppAds.pdf.

PurdueSports.com (2011, September 23). Social media night: Get in the game. Retrieved from http://www.purduesports.com/sports/w-volley/spec-rel/092311aag.html.

Rubin, C. (2011, January 27). Consumers wary of location-based services. Retrieved from http://www.inc.com/news/articles/2011/01/users-have-uneasy-relationship-with-location-based-services.html.

Siwicki, B. (2011, June 15). IRCE 2011 report: More mobile devices means more shopping, a survey finds. Retrieved from http://www.internetretailer.com/2011/06/15/irce-2011-report-more-mobile-devices-means-more-shopping.

Smith, A. (2011, September 19). Americans and text messaging. Pew Internet and American Life Project. Retrieved from http://pewinternet.org/Reports/2011/Cell-Phone-Texting-2011.aspx.

Smith, A. (2012, June 26). Cell internet use 2012. *Pew Internet and American Life Project*. Retrieved from http://pewinternet.org/Reports/2012/Cell-Internet-Use-2012.aspx.

Tsirulnik, G. (2010, October 22). ESPN is mobile publisher of the year. Retrieved from http://www.mobilemarketer.com/cms/news/media/7846.html.

Zickuhr, K., & Smith, A. (2010, November 4). 4% of online Americans use location-based services. Retrieved from http://pewinternet.org/Reports/2010/Location-based-services.aspx.

CHAPTER 8

Email Marketing

INTRODUCTION

In order to succeed in today's fast-paced world, businesses need to build and maintain strong communication channels with customers. One of the most cost-effective tools used to engage current customers and develop new ones is email marketing. According to Internet World Stats (2012), more than 77 percent of the estimated 311 million people in the United States use online resources. Of those who use the Internet, 95 percent use email. However, according to the same source, the U.S. is dwarfed by Asia and Europe when it comes to sheer numbers of Internet users. As of June 2012, Asia had more than 1 billion Internet users, while Europe totaled more than 518 million users.

With such a high percentage of people using the Internet and marketers increasingly focusing on developing better and more measurable communications, targeted email is a natural fit for marketers. Email marketing is a cost-effective way to deliver targeted messages to customers and prospects. Sport marketers often focus on core key messages in these communications including team history, education about the organization and the sport, ticket and promotional offers, discounts, as well as content links that drive traffic back to the team's website. Additionally, email marketing provides tracking options for each campaign and customer through links provided in the email, whose clicks can be measured.

EMAIL MARKETING DEFINED

Email marketing is an online marketing tool that allows custom and industry-specific content to be delivered to a targeted audience, the results of which can be measured. Purposes for email marketing include:

- Sending targeted and relevant email messages to existing customers to enhance the relationship and to encourage repeat business and customer loyalty.
- Sending email messages for the purpose of acquiring new customers or convincing current customers to purchase something immediately.
- Delivering value-added advertising and links for corporate sponsors within an email marketing campaign.
- Delivering valuable content to an existing database to keep customers engaged with the brand.

Let's say a college football program wants to communicate with its entire season ticket database. Using an email marketing program, the university's sport marketing team can reach out to this loyal and targeted audience with important news, such as the new football schedule, the payment plan for the coming year, and dates for the opening of spring practice. During the off-season, these same core customers can be targeted to purchase football merchandise as well as exclusive offers not available to the general public.

Furthermore, the department may want to increase its fan base, recognizing that casual fans without season tickets may also want up-to-date information on the program regarding the latest signees or notice of discounted tickets for future home games. The fan provides a means to contact the football program (his or her email address) and permission to do so, while the front office is granted the opportunity to communicate in a meaningful way.

In order to achieve these goals, sport organizations can create email programs to communicate with these market segments. They send out information, often to large groups, to people who have requested it. These large group emails are known as *blasts* or *eblasts* because they are essentially a formatted email that is "blasted" over the Internet to a target group.

The eMarketing Association

The eMarketing Association (eMA) is an organization that promotes email marketing. According to their website, www.emarketingassociation.com, this group is "the world's largest international association of eMarketing professionals. Members include governments, companies, professionals and students involved with the emarketing arena. The eMA provides marketing resources, services, research, certifications, educational programs and events to its members and the marketing community" (eMA, n.d.). The eMA works with a number of organizations, companies, and government agencies on issues related to ecommerce, multichannel marketing, and legislative issues. Full-time students receive a discount for a one-year membership. Membership includes various discounts, the eMA newsletter, and access to a members-only area with industry-related resources.

COLLECTING EMAIL ADDRESSES

Who do teams and other sport organizations email? Their established customer base, naturally. This includes casual fans and season ticket holders, customers who have purchased goods, and clients—anyone who has provided an email address. If an individual appears in the organization's contact database, they have likely shared their email address at some point. This point of contact might have come from a ticket purchase, newsletter sign-up, promotional contest, or opt-in email campaign. For example, a team might be trying to drive revenue with a special family ticket plan, which may include tickets and food and drink at a special price. Contacting fans with a compelling message via email is a practical and cost-effective way to meet revenue goals.

Potential new fans and customers are also a target for email marketing campaigns. However, the organization is less likely to have email addresses for this group. This adds an additional challenge to such a campaign.

Email Signups

Many sport organizations offer fans and customers an opportunity to sign up for email communications via their websites, as shown in Exhibit 8.1. Smart organizations provide links for email communications "above the fold" on the home page of the website. Placement in the upper half of the web page is ideal for promoting database capture. The link then connects to a brief form that gives the organization permission to email the consumer and captures important data such as city, state,

EXHIBIT 8.1   Email and other communication options on the Chicago Blackhawks website.

The Chicago Blackhawks homepage offers fans a variety of ways to stay connected including linking to Facebook, Twitter and signing up for an email marketing newsletter or e-news. Once fans click on this link, they are then offered the opportunity to sign up for one of two online newsletters: a weekly *Red & White* newsletter or a game day marketing blast called *Blackhawks Gameday*.

Source: Blackhawks.nhl.com. Used with permission.

and phone number. A consumer who is willing to provide both a phone number and an email address can now be contacted regarding sales and promotions (tickets, suites, sports memorabilia) via two different methods. The data can be stored in a central database by the software provider and can be accessed online or downloaded at any time.

Other ways to collect data to drive email marketing communications include online and offline enter-to-win contests, free product samplings in exchange for filling out forms, and asking for an address when purchasing tickets or merchandise either online or offline.

One popular method to acquire this data is by creating contests on an organization's website or a popular social media platform, such as Facebook, to drive additional fans to a centralized database. For example, during the 2011 season, the NFL's New England Patriots created a "Verizon

EXHIBIT 8.2   One benefit of promotions is collecting email addresses.

NFL Trivia Live" contest. What would entice fans to play online? The site offered daily prizes, including tickets to Super Bowl XLVI. The only cost to the fans was investing time to play the trivia contest and providing an email address (see Exhibit 8.2). For the team, it proved to be a cost-effective tool to acquire new customers to direct their email marketing efforts.

Yet another tool used to acquire new user information is team-specific content. The University of Southern California Trojans, for example, offer exclusive content, including interviews, stories, and research to fans who enter a valid email address when signing up online for information on a specific team. The California-based school offers nearly two dozen categories, allowing fans to customize the information they want to receive by filling out a few fields and hitting the send button.

Marketers must examine all of their communication tools and efforts to ensure they are designed to collect customer data whenever possible. This includes providing links within company email signatures, on-site questionnaires, and having staff members fill in missing email addresses when making calls to clients. However, sport marketers need to recognize that email marketing is permission-based communication. Contacts need to consensually provide their email in order for a team or business to communicate with them on an ongoing basis. This is also known as opt-in or permission-based marketing. Once the opt-in is completed, the visitor officially becomes an approved subscriber. The team or business can begin sending targeted messages.

There is no special wording for this permission. Providing an area where the subscriber can enter his/her name, email address, and categories for preferred types of communication works well.

As shown in Exhibit 8.3, the USC form allows users to sign up for one or more emails depending on the sport. USC keeps the email lists for these topics separated so the messages can be tailored and the overall message will not be diluted with unwanted emails. For example, women's basketball boosters may not want to receive a men's water polo email.

EXHIBIT 8.3   Allowing users to customize content.

Trojans   The Official E-Mail of USC Athletics

SC   **VICTORY**MAIL
Presented by **YP**

First Name
Last Name
Email Address

Send me these recurring emails: ☑ All Emails

☐ This Week at Troy – weekly on-campus sporting events
☐ The State of Troy - monthly email from Pat Haden on topics of interest
☐ Trojan Voices – monthly newsletter focusing on off field Trojan exploits

Send me sport specific communications: ☑ All Sports
Updates may include ticket information, sport updates and special event invitations

☐ Football   ☐ Men's Basketball
☐ Men's Volleyball   ☐ Women's Basketball
☐ Women's Volleyball   ☐ Baseball
☐ Soccer   ☐ Water Polo
☐ Tennis   ☐ Swimming & Diving
☐ Track & Field   ☐ Golf
☐ Rowing   ☐ Lacrosse

☑ Send me special offers and giveaways from USC and corporate partners

[Submit]

Source: USC Trojans website, http://www.usctrojans.com/ot/pac-mail.html. Used with permission.

Marketers that merge distinct lists may upset customers and cause problems. Thus, USC and all successful marketers work to keep specific lists separate and well documented.

EMAIL CAMPAIGNS

An organization may conduct many different types of email marketing campaigns depending on its goals. One campaign may use a professional-looking online newsletter to deliver updates and interesting stories. Another may choose to educate its audience about the organization or team, its culture, and history while another may be designed to sell products or services, branded items, or sponsorships while promoting upcoming events.

Before beginning an email campaign, have a goal clearly in mind: What do you hope to accomplish with this particular email? Generate new revenue sources, deliver news, or maybe grow the user database? Sometimes it may be the general goal of remaining visible to the consumer, but more often there is a specific goal. For example, you may want to introduce new products or services, announce a change, invite consumers to a specific event, and so forth. The form and content of your message will be directly related to its purpose.

Just as important as identifying the purpose of the email is to identify the audience you want to reach. Sometimes that will be your entire email list; other times you may be reaching out to a specific group of individuals (season ticket holders, people registered for a particular fitness program, and so forth). Write and revise your content based on both your goals and your audience.

Creating Emails for Campaigns

Once you've obtained people's email addresses and received permission to email them, the next step is to begin a dialogue. In order to determine the frequency of communication, you may want to create a yearly internal communication calendar and schedule time periods with specific topics for each communication.

While the goal behind the messages may vary, the quality must be consistently high. The consumer receiving the email must see value in your organization's messages that show up in their inbox. The more value you are able to deliver in each communication, the higher the chances are the fan or prospective customer will continue to open the email, read it, and act on it.

The actual email begins with the subject line. This phrase or sentence must be compelling enough to motivate the receiver to open the document. Email marketing provider iContact.com, in its Best Practices white paper (2009), suggests a range between 20 and 50 characters for an email subject line. By making the statement bold, interesting, and compelling, the subject line has a better opportunity to engage the recipient. Would you rather read an email that says "49ers Break Ground on New Stadium" or an email that says "October 49ers Newsletter"?

The actual content of the email may include the following, depending on its intended purpose:

1. Short briefs on each topic with a link to another destination that has more information, often the organization's website.
2. Images: Dress up the content with related photos and other graphics.
3. Video: Link to an outside source such as YouTube, your stored clips, or to other video sources.
4. Links to social media sites to help this community engage on a different platform. Popular destinations include Twitter, Facebook, and the team blog.
5. Coupons: If you are looking for activation, embed a coupon or extra value to make members take an action.

Ultimately, an organization's goal should be to turn a potentially passive form of communication into one that is more interactive and action-based. The first way to do this is to create links within the email for the targeted audience to click on. This changes a passive, one-way conversation with the reader into a two-way interaction that enables them to take an active role.

Let's say the Los Angeles Clippers are trying to increase ticket sales for a specific home game. Prior to the game, they might send an email that includes a brief story on the visiting team coming to Los Angeles as well as a link for fans to purchase the tickets after reading the story.

The second option is to include a forward button. Let's say a person who received the Clippers email is not able to attend the game, but she may want to let her die-hard basketball friends know about the event. This can be easily accomplished by inserting a forward link so that she can send the email directly to her friends.

Timing Your Communication

When it comes to a specific time and day to send electronic communication, that may vary depending on your audience and purpose. You may wish to experiment with send times and days, using analytics to judge the results. To offer a baseline: In a survey conducted of 100 business-to-business marketers by MarketingProfs.com (2012), 44 percent of respondents said that Tuesdays yielded the best results for open rates and 53 percent claimed Fridays were the worst. Fifty-four percent of these same respondents stated that the best time to send was between 8:00 a.m. and noon.

How Much Is Too Much?

An important question is: How often should I be contacting my database? What is the frequency needed to maintain and grow the relationship? One way to test for frequency effectiveness is to check message open rates during periods of frequent communications versus periods of infrequent communications.

If you send emails too often, you risk diluting the intended message and the impact you have on the overall campaign. You also risk fans choosing to stop receiving your emails entirely. By law, if consumers choose to stop receiving emails or opt-out of email communication, you must take them off your contact email database. Remember, they gave you permission to email and they can take it away at any time. If they choose to leave this communication platform, you can no longer communicate via this channel any further. Your email may also be seen as spam, which we will discuss below.

On the other hand, if you do not communicate often enough with your customers, you are not building a relationship to meet their needs. To build a relationship, your communication needs to provide information, insight, and opportunity:

- **Information:** Customers who have opted-in for this reason are not getting enough information elsewhere, so they came directly to you. Now provide it! In addition to fans and customers, you might develop an informational email blast to vendors, sponsors, or key city-wide partners.

- **Insight:** Where better to learn in-depth insider information than from the organization directly?

- **Opportunity:** You have their attention, now how can you use it to your advantage across the entire business unit? Cross-sell with opportunities that your customers may not have thought about or been exposed to in the past. For example, a company that operates and owns a sport team may choose to cross-sell an upcoming concert by sending special ticket information to the sports database.

Avoiding Opt-Outs and Being Labeled as Spam

While *opt-in* is the term for someone who gives you permission to send her email, *opt-out* is the term for when a subscriber to your email marketing list decides she wants no further communication with your organization.

Think about what a subscriber's typical action might be when she wants to opt-out from receiving email communications. A leading email marketing company, Exact Target (2011), shared these reasons from their study:

- 67% said they would click on the "unsubscribe" button.
- 17% said they would delete the emails when they arrive.
- 8% said they would click on the spam or junk mail option.
- 6% reported they would do nothing, just ignore the emails.
- 2% said they would set up a filter. (A filter is a rule set up in an email program that can block email messages based on the subject line, email address, or name and address listed in the email itself.)

If your email is labeled as spam, it won't reach your target audience. Spam is junk email sent to a large group of people. In the early days of the Internet this practice was not regulated, but now it is. The Federal Trade Commission's Can-Spam Act (2003) sets rules for commercial emails and also allows users to stop a company from sending future emails they no longer wish to receive. This law requires email marketers not to use misleading or deceptive subject lines, include a real physical address for where the communication originates, and provide information about how to opt-out of future emails. Failing to comply with these rules is punishable by up to $16,000 for every email sent to subscribers who opt-out of communications.

Email marketing, like spam, does send the same message to a large group of people. However, if the recipient deems the content valuable, then chances are it won't be labeled as spam. Any individual can inform his or her email provider via a simple click that a commercial email is spam. One or two of these might not change your status, but a slew of comments could get your company banned from using this service. In order to avoid being labeled a spammer, content providers must deliver valuable information without asking too much from the recipient.

Using certain terms in email communication can also cause your email to wind up in a spam folder. Phrases such as "Act now," "Save up to," and "You've been selected" are often labeled as spam (iContact, 2009).

A few years ago, marketers were able to send an email to a large group of people from a personal account. After limits to the number of email addresses included in a single email were placed on Internet service providers, new companies formed to tackle this challenge. Today, companies such as iContact, Constant Contact, and Exact Target work with businesses to conform to spam rules and maintain customer verification.

EMAIL MARKETING STRATEGIES

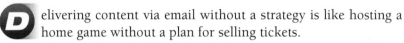 elivering content via email without a strategy is like hosting a home game without a plan for selling tickets.

The first step is to develop a plan for the content you want to deliver. It may be information regarding season ticket renewals or sponsorship activation programs or feature stories on popular players, new activity programs, and community-related events. Once you have identified your list of items, analyze it in regard to the calendar. Ask yourself, What will take place each month and how can you plan to stay visible during less-busy months or the off-season?

Once the editorial calendar is complete, begin developing the content to match the calendar. This process, from identifying topics through writing and producing the content, is much like what a traditional magazine publisher or editor would do. The reality is that you, the developer of email for a marketing program, have become the publisher of your own news and information to distribute to those who want to receive it.

Brian Anthony Hernandez (2011), a writer for Mashable.com, offers "Six Smart and Effective Email Marketing Tactics" for users. Here they are adapted for the sports industry:

1. **Tap into current events and pop culture.** Active fans that follow a specific team are more likely to react to an email that mentions current team-related news or a big anniversary of a significant event that has happened related to the team, such as winning a division championship.

2. **Use Twitter and Facebook to promote opt-in URLs.** Use integrated marketing campaigns, meaning different platforms of online and offline communication tools, to deliver the same key messages to users across a variety of verticals. Many popular online social media tools have large followings that help drive traffic back to a sign-up page. The page will allow an organization to engage fans and capture their contact information.

3. **Segment your contact database.** Sending messages that are targeted to the wrong audience will not only upset them, but may also prompt them to unsubscribe so you will never be able to contact them again. It is important to know their interests and what they want to hear. The more information you have on what they want to receive from you, the better the chances are that they will continue to react to your targeted messages.

4. **Provide incentives to email subscribers via social media.** Fans and clients of sport organizations have a real passion for favorite players, coaches, fitness, activities, stadiums, and so forth. It is easy to envision using autographs, appearances, discounted programs, and other incentives to help motivate them to read, click, and respond to your targeted email.

5. **Expand email lists with SMS promotion.** SMS is used by organizations today with a brief code number that allows consumers to punch in a number to opt-in to an email marketing list.

6. **Optimize emails for smartphones.** Smartphones are a part of many fans' daily lives. Since their email travels with them, your messages need to be formatted for mobile devices for the best results.

MEASUREMENT

Marketing also involves measuring, and email marketing has become the marketer's go-to technology for better understanding the relationship between content and the fan's interest in it. In terms of tools to activate an audience, email marketing ranks high in effectiveness and in measurability (we'll discuss this more in Chapter 9). Let's take a print ad that appears in *Sports Illustrated.* This legendary publication can tell you how many subscribers receive the magazine and where they are located. But they cannot tell you how many people actually opened the magazine and read the advertisement. *Sports Illustrated* also cannot tell you how many people took action on your ad. Email marketing bridges this gap via technology.

According to research conducted by Experian Simmons (2011), Internet users in the United States were more likely to click on links embedded in marketing emails than in other online marketing formats such as banners or online video advertisements (see Exhibit 8.4).

A key advantage in email marketing measurement is that feedback is immediate. If the Dallas Cowboys send out a season ticket renewal form by traditional mail, the effectiveness of the campaign

EXHIBIT 8.4   Frequency of clicking on select online marketing formats according to U.S. adult Internet users (Sept. 2010).

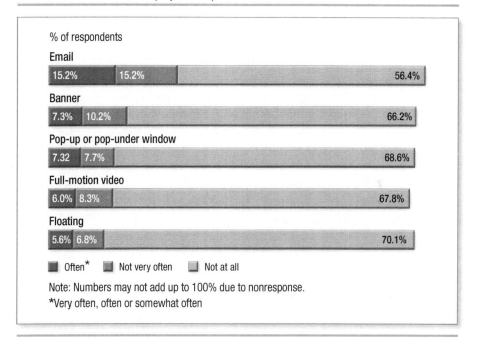

% of respondents

Email
| 15.2% | 15.2% | 56.4% |

Banner
| 7.3% | 10.2% | 66.2% |

Pop-up or pop-under window
| 7.32 | 7.7% | 68.6% |

Full-motion video
| 6.0% | 8.3% | 67.8% |

Floating
| 5.6% | 6.8% | 70.1% |

■ Often* ■ Not very often □ Not at all

Note: Numbers may not add up to 100% due to nonresponse.
*Very often, often or somewhat often

Source: Used with permission of eMarketer.com. Data from Experian Simmons, National consumer study, Feb. 16, 2011.

would be measured over a period of several weeks by the number of customers who called the sales department to renew their seats. By using an email marketing program, however, the Cowboys can identify who has received the email, who opened it, who clicked on specific links, and who paid for their renewals online, all in real time.

Dashboard Data

With email campaigns, clicks, forwards, spam clicks, as well as email bounces or bad addresses can all be measured. When using an email service provider such as Lyris, Exact Target, or iContact, proprietary software tracks the interaction process. For example, each time a person opens an email, this action is recorded by the email provider. The provider makes the tracking information viewable on a customized data information page or online dashboard. It is often recorded by both the total number of "opens" as well as by percentage rate based on the total number of people contacted. An email's open rate is the percentage of recipients who opened an email compared to how many were sent the email. This percentage is calculated to exclude bounces, or emails sent that were unsuccessful in reaching their intended inbox. The percentage of opens is calculated by dividing the number of unique opens by the number of emails sent, excluding the number of bounces.

Open rates are an important measure of email campaign's success and a key reason why email marketing is so popular. Imagine sending a regular email to a prospect that promotes an upcoming hockey game in your arena. Without the ability to measure if they received it and opened it, you may as well be sending a letter via the post office.

Click-through rates, or CTRs, can also be measured. CTRs represent the percentage of opens that result in clicks on the links in a given email marketing campaign. Perhaps the most important rate is the conversion rate, which refers to the percentage of readers of a given email campaign that become paying customers as a result of an advertising effort. For example, percentages will reflect those who clicked through to the links and those who performed the intended action (e.g., purchase a product, sign up for a newsletter, and so forth).

A natural question after you have sent out an email to your targeted list is, was this campaign effective? Most industry email marketers track effectiveness of client campaigns across a variety of industry categories, but a general rule for a successful open rate is right around 20 percent of the total number of emails successfully delivered. This information is useful for several reasons. Knowing that a specific person clicked on a link such as one that provides suite information might help the sales team follow up in a timely manner to close a sale.

Lastly, if the content is irrelevant or too frequent, your emails may be labeled spam. An organization receiving too many "opt-outs" in this manner may lose its ability to use email marketing with a provider. It is important to benchmark and measure opt-out rates. Benchmarking allows you to gauge changes over time, to determine if the rates are growing, staying the same, or declining. This is measured the same way an open rate is measured. The results are reflected in the dashboard by total numbers who have chosen this path and as a percentage of the total population who received the individual email campaign.

CONCLUSION

 mail marketing is an important tool in the overall marketing mix that can educate and engage current customers and key clients. Email technology can also be used to collect and expand current databases for prospecting new customers and selling tickets, sponsorships, and merchandise. Marketing departments must understand how to use this tool, the value of delivering good content, and how often to contact people for maximum effectiveness.

REVIEW QUESTIONS

1. How does email marketing differ from traditional communication tools like print advertising?
2. What is an eblast?
3. Why should marketers know about the Can-Spam law?
4. Name several ways marketers can measure the impact of email marketing.

REFERENCES

eMA (n.d.). About the eMarketing Association. Retrieved from http://www. emarketingassociation.com/about.htm.

ExactTarget.com (2011). The social break-up: A subscribers, fans, and followers research report. http://www.exacttarget.com/Resources/SFF8.pdf?et_cid= 37725522&et_rid=1482815418&linkid=Download+The+Social+Break-Up+Now.

Experian Simmons (2011, Feb. 16). National consumer study. eMarketer.com. Retrieved from http://www.experian.com/simmons-research/consumer-study.html.

Federal Trade Commission (2003). Can-Spam Act: A compliance guide for businesses. http://www.business.ftc.gov/documents/bus61-can-spam-act-compliance-guide-business.

Hernandez, B. A. (2011, April 19). Six smart & effective email marketing tactics. Mashable.com. Retrieved from http://mashable.com/2011/04/19/email-marketing-tactics.

iContact (2009). Best practices for email marketing. Available: http://www. icontact.com/static/pdf/Email_Marketing_Best_Practices_iContact.pdf.

Internet World Stats (2012a). Usage and population statistics, United States. http://www.internetworldstats.com/unitedstates.htm.

Internet World Stats (2012b). Internet users in the world, distribution by world regions, 2012, Q2. http://www.internetworldstats.com/unitedstates.htm.

MarketingProfs.com (2012). B2B email marketing best-practices and trends. http://www.marketingprofs.com/charts/2012/8524/b2b-email-marketing-best-practices-and-trends#ixzz2HvH70Vc2.

Planning and Measuring a Successful Social Media Program

INTRODUCTION

By now you've learned many social media basics and how social tools, channels, and platforms are affecting sport marketing. You've read about content such as pictures, video, and real-time updates. You've seen examples of how sport organizations are using social tools and platforms and learned some best practices for how to utilize them. In this final chapter, we cover how to plan a social media program and measure its effectiveness.

The ability of a company to measure the effectiveness of a social media campaign is much debated. Some say that social media is impossible to measure, because it is not really a direct sales channel. Others argue that social media is an essential business technology, and that trying to measure the effects of social media is like trying to measure the effects of the phone or a fax machine—it isn't even worth discussing.

One thing is for certain—social media is definitely not free, even if many of its tools and platforms are. It takes time, money, and resources to effectively plan, implement, manage, and assess social media programs.

Because social media programs require an investment, organizations must be able to justify this investment and measure its outcomes.

Sport marketers must be knowledgeable about the measurement of social media, so we can justify the use of social tools (and the resources and time they require) and explain the results to bosses, coworkers, clients, and sponsors. Studies show, for example, that "sports fans who follow their favorite athletes on social media are 55% more likely to purchase a brand if an athlete mentions it on Facebook or Twitter" (Werner, 2011). But we still have to prove positive results in our own programs.

In this chapter we cover the basics of planning a campaign and provide information on a few different ways to think about measurement. We also look at examples of elements that can be measured and some important measurement tools. Lastly, we go over a few best practices for optimizing your programs and campaigns and explore some challenges of measuring the effectiveness of social media programs.

PLANNING A SUCCESSFUL SOCIAL MEDIA PROGRAM

Measurement is an important part of any social media initiative, but it is still just one piece of an overall program. Before diving into measurement, you must already have a strong foundation in place for the overall social media program. First, ask why your organization has a social media program in the first place. This will ensure that the program is properly aligned with the organization's business objectives. Then, the program's effectiveness can be measured by how well it meets these business objectives.

Crafting A Strategy: The POST Method

Forrester Research's POST method (Bernoff, 2007) offers some great insights into the basics of social media strategy. Its simple approach is based on four key components: (1) people, (2) objectives, (3) strategy, and (4) technology.

People

The first step in any social media program involves audience research. This ensures that the program is designed to resonate with the target audience. In this phase, the goal is to understand:

- What social media websites and platforms people are using to communicate about your brand and related topics.

- What people are saying about your brand and related topics, and what types of content are most popular with your audience.

- What topics are most popular with your audience.

- What the demographics are of the people talking about your brand and key topics online.

- How people are sharing content about your brand and key topics online.

- How your audience is interacting with each other online, with you, and with similar organizations.

One method for obtaining this information is to hire an outside marketing agency and tell them what you want to understand. A good agency (especially one that has expertise with social media) should be able to do this. You can find a listing of social media agencies in InvestInSocial.com, a directory that lists a variety of social media agencies, vendors, and consultants.

The other way to gather this information is for an organization to do it on its own. Start by surveying your audience to gain a better understanding of people's online behavior and preferences. A social media monitoring tool, such as Radian6 or Sysomos MAP, can be very helpful in this research. These monitoring tools can tell you where your target audience is talking, what they're saying about you, what the sentiments of the discussions are, and what the volume of conversation is. They can also provide some helpful demographic and topical information about these online discussions. Alternatively, organizations can also use a mix of free tools, such as Google Analytics, Google Blogsearch, and Twitter search, as a supplement to these paid tools or as a substitute for paid tools, if your organization's budget is tight. For example, a team might search for its name and other main keywords in Twitter to see what people on the service are saying about them. Having some research and insight is always better than having no research, especially when it comes to understanding your audience before moving onto the next phase of social media strategy.

Objectives

Next, an organization should decide on an objective for its social media program. The program may have one main objective (e.g., increase brand awareness), or there may be multiple objectives (e.g., increase brand awareness, monitor what people are saying to improve the effectiveness of future marketing campaigns, and increase sales). This objective can be financial (e.g., selling more merchandise online) or psychological (e.g., changing fan perceptions about a league). Whatever your objective, establishing it is a crucial step—one that many organizations overlook. If an organization doesn't know what it is trying to accomplish with social media, it won't develop the proper tactics to support the program. It also won't be able to determine if its program is successful. Choosing an objective (or multiple objectives) is essential for an overall social media program and for any individual, short-term campaigns.

How do you decide on an objective? Objectives for social media marketing programs should align with overall business and marketing goals. These goals can vary based on if the strategy is for a team, athlete, sport brand, or other sports company. An athlete may be looking to expand his or her online presence to appear more attractive to potential sponsors. A retail sports brand may want to increase sales and market share. A sport-related nonprofit organization may be trying to reach more potential donors and increase the dollar amount that it is receiving from current donors. Ultimately, the goal should reflect whatever the organization or individual is trying to achieve.

Strategy

After the objectives are determined, strategy can be developed. According to Forrester's Josh Bernoff (2007), strategy involves addressing how a social media program will change an organization or individual's relationship with the audience:

> Strategy here means figuring out what will be different after you're done. Do you want a closer, two-way relationship with your best customers? Do you want to get people talking about your products? Do you want a permanent focus group for testing product ideas and generating new ones? Imagine you succeed. How will things be different afterwards? (unpaged)

See Exhibit 9.1 for an example of how objectives and basic strategy could work together for a fictional baseball team, the Arlington Riders.

As part of this strategy, organizations should address a few questions, including the following:

- When, how, and where will we engage our audience?
- How will we proactively AND reactively engage with our audience?

EXHIBIT 9.1   Sample social media strategy plan for the Arlington Riders.

Objective: Increase ticket sales.

Secondary objective: Increase online conversation about the team.

Strategy: Increase engagement with fans on Twitter and Facebook and build the team's following on each site to increase reach and awareness of the team. Convert Facebook fans and Twitter followers into new customers and empower them to spread the word about the team to their friends on these websites.

- What kind of content will need to be created, and who will create it?
- How often should content be created?
- What resources and time will it take to execute this program?
- How will we promote our social media program through other channels, such as our website and email newsletter?

Keep in mind that this strategy should always be aligned with whatever objective(s) the organization has agreed upon.

Technology

The final step in Forrester's POST method for social strategy is deciding which social technologies to use. Based on research about your audience, the objectives of your program, and your strategy for achieving these goals, you should now be able to decide which social media technologies you will need.

When evaluating the various platforms and technologies that are available, consider the strengths of each platform and think about how they align with your objectives and strategy. For example, an organization may discover that its audience is interested in entertaining videos and sharing them with friends. One of the organization's objectives may be to expand its reach, particularly among casual fans. The organization then decides that it needs to find a way to expose casual fans to entertaining content that they will want to share with their friends. Based on these initial steps, the organization determines that it should utilize YouTube as the main hub for its entertaining video content.

Forrester's POST method for social strategy is a great starting point for sport marketers who are serious about planning, implementing, and measuring a successful social media program. However, two additional aspects of social media strategy are crucial to a successful initiative and help lay additional groundwork for measuring the campaign's effectiveness.

Crafting a Strategy: Targets and Tactics

While the *T* in Forrester's POST process stands for *technology*, it is important for sport marketers to consider two other *T*s when planning a successful social media program: targets and tactics. We'll explore each of these briefly.

Targets

According to Olivier Blanchard (2011a), author of *Social Media ROI: Managing and Measuring Social Media Efforts in Your Organization*, "setting goals and objectives is not enough. In order to drive toward a specific result (a desired result), an organization must set targets" (p. 17). Setting targets involves taking an organization's objectives with a social media program and creating specific definitions of success. Blanchard (2011a) defines a target as "the specific value assigned to an objective within a finite timeframe" (p. 15). In the process of planning a successful social media program, targets should help drive an organization toward success. Here are a few examples of targets that an organization might set:

- Add 100 new, first-time donors in three months.
- Generate 100,000 views of a sponsor's videos in six months.
- Increase sales of merchandise from referral traffic from Facebook 20 percent in one year.
- Increase positive mentions on Twitter 30 percent in one year.

Establishing specific targets helps make social media objectives a reality. It also ensures that the people involved in an organization's social media program can be held accountable for the results and thus become invested in the program's success.

Tactics

Outlining specific tactics is the final crucial part of planning a successful social media program. According to Blanchard (2011a), "tactics are the means by which a strategy may be carried out . . . tactics are the methods used on the ground to execute a strategy" (p. 15). The tactics will explain the specific actions that are needed to support the organization's strategy.

EXHIBIT 9.2   Combining objectives, targets, strategy, and tactics.

Objective: Increase ticket sales.

Target: Sell tickets to 100 first-time buyers in the next three months.

Strategy: Reach new ticket buyers through current Facebook fans and Twitter followers, and empower current followers to share team-related content and offers.

Tactics: Reward the first 20 Twitter followers who retweet designated content each week with two discounts on tickets—one discount that they can use and one that they can share with a friend. Promote "Bring a Facebook Friend Nights" on Facebook page and let people enter a sweepstakes to win free tickets to give their friends.

See Exhibit 9.2 for an example of how an objective, target, strategy, and supporting tactics can work together as part of a team's social media plan.

When thinking about these tactics, organizations should consider the time and resources it will take to implement them. Every organization is different, but one way to estimate time requirements is by looking at what it will take to have people respond to mentions about the organization. Many organizations spend a great amount of time reacting to what people are saying about them. One way to estimate how much time this will take is by looking at the number of times people are mentioning an organization each day and then how long it takes the organization to respond to each mention, on average.

Now that you've seen how to plan a successful social media program and defined what success would mean to your organization, you're ready to learn about measuring the effectiveness of your social media efforts and determine whether you've achieved that success.

APPROACHES TO SOCIAL MEDIA MEASUREMENT

As we mentioned previously, there is much debate about how to measure social media effectiveness, and whether it can be measured at all. From our experience, many companies—both in and out of sports—are not really measuring their social media initiatives. Other companies may be measuring things such as Twitter followers or Facebook likes, without putting much thought into how that is related to their overall business goals. Sheldon Levine, community manager for Sysomos, a company that provides social media software, says that "social media is new and shiny, but don't let the shininess distract you from [it] being a real business with real business goals" (Manjoo, 2011, unpaged).

Before we go any further, let's make sure you're familiar with a key measurement term: return on investment (ROI). This is a metric that is used to calculate the efficiency of an investment. It's calculated like this:

ROI = (Gain from investment − Cost of investment) / Cost of investment

ROI is typically expressed as a percentage. For example, if you invested $1,000 into a marketing program and generated $2,000 in new profits, your ROI would be 1, or 100 percent. If you invested the same amount of money and only generated $800 in new profits, your ROI would be 20 percent. Obviously, companies want a positive ROI from programs on which they spend money.

Just because many organizations do not measure the ROI or the effectiveness of their social media programs, does not mean it can't be done. Although the industry has no standard way to measure the effectiveness of these programs, the following two approaches are useful.

Direct ROI

The ideal way to measure social media effectiveness is to use the direct ROI model. Kevin Briody, director of strategic partnerships for Ignite Social Media, says that "direct ROI is where you can directly track the impact your social media activities have on increasing revenue, reducing costs, or both" (2011, unpaged). The direct ROI model is best used for social media initiatives that offer consumers opportunities to make a direct transaction as a result of some type of content posted to a social media website. An example of this is when a nonprofit organization uses its tweets to encourage people to donate, or when a team includes a link to purchase tickets at the end of each video it posts on YouTube. See Exhibit 9.3 for an example of a Facebook update from the Washington Nationals that encourages people to make a purchase. Using the appropriate tracking software, the team can track sales back to this specific channel.

The direct ROI model allows an organization to calculate exactly what went into a social media program, what it got out of it, and the program's return. This is usually expressed in the form of dollars. The investment may include a certain number of hours per week

EXHIBIT 9.3   Washington Nationals Facebook update.

Washington Nationals
School's out, Nats fans! Celebrate with 20% off kids gear at the
Nationals.com Shop.

   **20% off wide variety of kids gear**
shop.mlb.com
Offer ends 6/27/11 at 11:59 pm ET

 June 21 at 1:32pm · Share

from an employee, which can be converted into a dollar amount based
on the employee's salary and added to the other costs associated with
the program.

While social media is not necessarily best utilized as a direct sales
channel, organizations can drive people to make purchases through
social platforms and channels. For example, in May 2007, Dell started
the "DellOutlet" Twitter account as a way to let people know when new
discounted products are added to its online outlet store. "We thought,
'Great—this has a really short lead time, and it will let us communicate
our message effectively,'" said Stefanie Nelson, manager of demand
generation at Dell Outlet (Bent Curve Media, n.d.). Dell began posting
updates a few times a week and tracking the URLs contained in them
so they could look at clicks and purchases to better understand what
people wanted.

After a year and a half, the company had generated more than $1
million in revenue from these sale alerts posted to Twitter (Schroeder,
2008). At the end of 2009, the company said it had generated more
than $6.5 million in revenue from these tweets (Ostrow, 2009). Dell
has shown that real revenue can be made from social media, and an
initiative like this can be successful.

When utilizing the direct ROI model to measure social media effectiveness, keep in mind this observation from Ignite Social Media's
Briody: "It's rare when you are going to calculate the ROI on a single
campaign in isolation, as the point of calculating ROI is not simply to
determine if an activity was financially worthwhile, but was it more or
less worthwhile relative to other possible marketing activities" (2011,
unpaged). This means that when looking at the ROI of a social media
program, you may want to compare it to the ROI of other programs.

For example, if an organization is looking to drive ticket sales through banner ads and through social media efforts, it should look at the ROI of each program to see which one was more cost effective and successful. After all, most programs are part of your larger marketing plan and you need to understand how they fit in that bigger picture.

The direct ROI model for social media measurement is a great model to use when a directly trackable benefit can be measured from a social media program, such as a purchase. However, this may not always be the case. The sales process may be complicated in some cases, such as when obtaining a new sponsor or selling corporate suites. Or a social media program may have multiple objectives (some of which may not be financial). In this case, the direct ROI of a program may be difficult to prove and correlated ROI may come into play.

Correlated ROI

When it is difficult or impossible to directly attribute sales or conversions to a social media program, organizations can look at possible correlations between their social media activities and the performance of key business metrics over a given time period. According to Briody (2011), "you're looking for statistically significant correlation between the two data sets, with an ideal of being to identify that for a given investment in social media efforts, or a given level of activity, you'll get a corresponding impact on a key business metric like sales." For sport organizations, this means looking at social media activities and business metrics together to see if any correlation can be drawn between the two.

In using the correlated ROI model of measurement, a sport organization may track things such as the number of overall followers and subscribers it has on Twitter, Facebook, and YouTube and the referral traffic from those websites to see if there is any correlation between increased sales of merchandise or tickets. A local beverage sponsor, for example, could see if there is any correlation between the number of times the sport property mentions it on Twitter and increased beverage sales at the event.

Another area to look at as part of this measurement model is purchase frequency and loyalty. For example, a retail sporting goods company could examine whether there is any correlation between the number of online mentions it receives across Twitter, blogs, and other social networks, and the average number of purchases customers make in a certain time period. A team could look at the purchase habits of fans that engage with them via social media compared with those who do not. For example, are fans who follow a team on Twitter and Facebook more likely to place multiple ticket orders than fans who do not follow the team on these sites? This could be a valuable correlation to identify, though acquiring this kind of information may require the use of surveys and additional research.

The correlated ROI model can be very beneficial in tracking the long-term effects of a social media program on the objectives the organization is trying to achieve. Because social media isn't always a channel that people turn to for immediate purchase decisions, and sport-related purchases may not always be made online, it may make more sense to look at the long-term impact a program can have on an organization's business goals and targets.

When using this approach, keep in mind that correlation does not imply causation. Just because an organization's Facebook likes have increased over the past six months and ticket sales have increased does not necessarily mean that the Facebook likes drove ticket sales. When utilizing this model, it's important to look at all of an organization's marketing programs to avoid falsely believing that one program's activities caused a certain outcome. For better or worse, it is usually not possible to prove true causation, because that would require looking at programs in isolation or even running only one type of marketing program at a time, which isn't feasible or even desirable for most organizations.

KEY PERFORMANCE INDICATORS

No matter which measurement approach an organization decides to take, it needs to determine what to measure before starting a new program. Hundreds of social media metrics can be tracked, but quantity doesn't always equate with quality or relevance. What matters is picking metrics that are aligned with the organization's objectives and targets. These metrics will be referred to as our key performance indicators (KPIs) for social media.

In his book *Social Media ROI*, Blanchard writes, "Key performance indicators illustrate the effectiveness of a campaign or program as it relates to hitting a specific target" (2011a, p. 32). KPIs are a *means to an end* (the end being the program's objectives and targets), not the end itself. For example, wanting to get 10,000 Facebook likes and 50 comments per day on your organization's Facebook wall is not a real business objective. However, the number of Facebook likes and comments can

EXHIBIT 9.4   How objectives, targets, and KPIs can work together for an adult soccer league.

Objective: Increase the number of adults registered for the fall season.

Target: 500 additional registrations before September 1.

KPIs: registrations prior to September 1.

- Clicks on links leading to videos about why people should play soccer.
- New likes on the league's Facebook page.
- New followers of the league's Twitter account.
- Increase in mentions about the league on Twitter.
- Number of comments left on the league's blog as part of a contest where people were encouraged to share what they love about the league.

be viewed as KPIs that are tracked to see if there's any correlation between these numbers and your progress toward the targets for a given campaign. Exhibit 9.4 gives an example of how objectives, targets, and KPIs can work together for an adult soccer league.

The KPIs an organization decides to measure will vary based on the social media program's objectives, targets, strategy, tactics, and timelines. As mentioned previously, it is vital that these KPIs are aligned with the program's goals. To help you identify various KPIs that may be valuable to track, consider the following four key KPI categories: (1) sales/revenues, (2) community size, (3) engagement, and (4) website metrics.

Sales/Revenue

While sales and revenue cannot always be measured directly, at times it makes sense to look at KPIs in this category, especially if one of the goals of the social media program is to drive people to complete a transaction online. Here are a few KPIs related to sales and revenue:

- Sales that were influenced by clicks on social content. If tracking is set up properly (more on this later in the chapter), this can include sales that result directly from clicks on social content as well as sales that may happen days or weeks later.
- Sales on items/offers that are unique to a specific social channel.
- Sales from website visitors (referral traffic) who came directly from a social media website, such as Facebook or Twitter.

- Conversion rates (number of website visitors who purchase something divided by the number of total unique website visitors in a given time period).

Community Size

The size of an organization's social media following—its community—can indicate how effective the program is. Here are some sample KPIs related to the size of an organization's online community:

- Facebook likes
- Twitter followers
- YouTube subscribers
- Blog subscribers
- Total community size (all subscribers/followers from multiple channels)

Engagement

The level of engagement an organization maintains with its audience can also help illustrate the effectiveness of a given social media program. Sport marketers can use the KPIs below to help quantify the level of online engagement around their brand:

- Retweets on Twitter
- Mentions on Twitter
- Comments on Facebook
- Average interactions (likes and comments) on Facebook per day
- Total online mentions of the brand within a given time period

Website Metrics

Website metrics can also yield valuable KPIs for an organization's social media program. These metrics include:

- Unique visitors
- The bounce rate, which is the percentage of visitors who enter the site and then leave the site—bounce—without viewing other pages
- Referral traffic from social networking websites
- Average time spent on the website
- Clicks on links (click-throughs)

The KPI examples outlined above should give you a good starting point for determining which metrics to track as part of your social media measurement process and how they relate to overall business objectives.

SOCIAL MEDIA MEASUREMENT TOOLS

nce you decide on your KPIs, you can start measuring them. This can even be done before starting a new social media program, as

C A S E   S T U D Y

The San Francisco Giants and Social Media

The San Francisco Giants got started with social media in 2010, and they use Facebook and Twitter to deliver real-time messages to fans. As of February 2013, the Giants have almost 1.7 million Facebook likes and 385,000 followers on Twitter. Bryan Srabian (2011), the team's director of social media, said that 2010 "was about growth. We wanted to figure out what people want."

By 2011, the Giants were still growing their community on Facebook and Twitter, but they were also focused on getting people to talk and interact more. They also looked at ticket sales. "It's nice to have lots of likes, but we're also trying to sell more tickets," Srabian said.

In 2011, one of the team's goals was to sell out all 81 home games, something it had done only in 2000, when the ballpark first opened (additional seats have been added to the stadium since then). Some games sold better than others, based on opponent, promotion, and day of week. It's also important to note that the Giants employ a dynamic pricing model, with ticket prices fluctuating with demand.

For a game between the Giants and the San Diego Padres on July 7th, about 2,000 tickets in a section had not been sold. On June 10—almost a month before the game—the team's ticketing department decided to cut ticket prices to seven dollars each and use social media channels to broadcast the discount. This decision was made at about 10:00 a.m., and by noon, the team had posted the offer on Facebook and Twitter for its fans. See Exhibit 9.5 for screenshots of these posts.

Within 24 hours, the Giants had sold out the tickets to fans through those two social media channels.

In this case, the team's goal was to sell the 2,000 extra tickets, which supported its overall objective for the season of selling out every home game. The tactics the Giants used were to post the discount on Facebook and Twitter, and the KPIs used were the number of tickets sold. As you can see, this promotion was a success.

EXHIBIT 9.5   San Francisco Giants promotion of the "Lucky7" ticket deal on Facebook and Twitter.

San Francisco Giants
$7 Tix - Giants vs Padres July 7th - #Lucky7 Ticket Offer - use coupon code seven - supply is limited http://atmlb.com/jNGUhq

7/7/$7 ticket offer (Lucky 7)

Don't miss the Giants vs Padres on July 7th at AT&T Park. Use code seven to get $7 tix while they last

@SFGiants
San Francisco Giants ✅

#Lucky7 Ticket offer - #SFGiants vs #Padres on 7/7 for just $7- Tix are going fast - use code seven
http://atmlb.com/iIqpXw

a way of gaining an understanding of the pre-campaign numbers. Let's take a look at some of the tools and software you may need to track them properly.

Website Analytics Software

All online measurement programs begin with website analytics. Some examples of this software include Google Analytics, Omniture, and Webtrends. As we mentioned in Chapter 4, these can help you measure just about everything visitors do on your website. This includes tracking what pages people are coming from, what pages people are viewing, and metrics related to ecommerce and conversions. These valuable programs help you track KPIs such as referral traffic from social networking websites and purchases resulting from this traffic. You can use this data to compare things such as bounce rates, conversion rates, and average pages viewed per visit and sales by those coming to the site via social media channels versus those who are coming from other sources.

The St. Patrick's Day Clippers Gold Contest

At the end of the 2010–2011 NBA season, the Los Angeles Clippers had a few objectives:

1. Increase registered users on its myClipper Nation fan engagement website (http://my.clippers.com/web/clippers/home).
2. Grow their potential season ticket leads.
3. Explore an opportunity with a potential new sponsor.

The team decided to work with GAGA Sports and Entertainment, a social media and customer relationship management (CRM) company that helps sport fans engage with brands, to create an online contest, the St. Patrick's Day Clippers Gold Contest, on its myClipper Nation website. From March 8th to 15th, fans could go to the website and enter to win a variety of prizes, including courtside tickets, an autographed team ball, and a bag with official team gear and autographed merchandise.

The Clippers promoted the contest through multiple channels online, beginning with its main website and their email newsletter. On Facebook and Twitter, the team posted four updates on each site about the contest, with links accompanying each update. The Clippers also used its Facebook profile picture and default Facebook tab to include branding about the contest. Lastly, the team worked with 2K Sports to be the presenting sponsor of this contest, satisfying one of their goals and getting the added benefit of having 2K Sports help promote the contest with four additional updates on Facebook and Twitter. See Exhibit 9.6 for examples of the updates the Clippers posted on Facebook and Twitter to promote this campaign.

The contest was a success and satisfied each of the team's objectives. The main KPIs tracked were the number of contest participants and the number of registered users on its myClipper Nation website. The Clippers reported that 2,600 people entered the contest, surpassing the 2,000 entries the team had estimated before launching the promotion, thus enabling the team to engage fans in a new way. The team also gained new leads for season ticket sales with 1,170 new users registered for its myClipper Nation website (National Sports Forum, 2011). And the team successfully partnered with a sponsor (2K Sports) to increase the program's reach and offer the sponsor unique access to fans.

EXHIBIT 9.6   Promotion of the St. Patrick's Day Clippers Gold Contest on Facebook and Twitter.

FACEBOOK UPDATES (4X with 2K Sports Mention)

Los Angeles Clippers

Want to win courtside tickets to watch Blake and the Clippers? How about a signed team ball? The St. Patrick's Day Clippers Gold Contest presented by 2K Sports is giving you the chance to win! Head over to myClipper NATION to enter! http://bit.ly/myclippers

TWITTER UPDATES (4X with 2K Sports Mention)

LAClippers Los Angeles Clippers

Want to win courtside tickets? Enter the St. Patrick's Day Clippers Gold Contest presented by @2KSports to win! http://bit.ly /myclippers

8 Mar

Basic Social Media Management and Tracking Software

When assessing your social media program, also consider software that helps you better manage your publishing and engagement efforts and track them to see what is working and what isn't working. Free software such as Tweetdeck and Hootsuite can help marketers improve productivity by managing all social media efforts within one dashboard or interface. These tools can be valuable in helping an organization schedule content to be posted on Facebook and Twitter, engage with a certain group of people (such as a company's most influential customers), and manage multiple social network accounts from one location. For instance, a team may have a ticket offer that it wants to post multiple times to Twitter (tweaking the copy each time to avoid being repetitive) and only once to Facebook. They also may want to set up a way to see all mentions about them and @ replies in real-time. This type of software can do all these things.

Organizations must also utilize a URL shortening/tracking solution. For example, a sponsor may want to know how many people clicked on a link. However, many links, especially to pages beyond the front page of a site, can be very long. A URL shortener such as Bitly can help. An original link such as http://www.thisisaveryveryveryverylonglink.com can be cleanly reduced to the shortened link http://bit.ly/jad.

Bitly.com and other such sites can help social media teams track clicks on links posted to Twitter, Facebook, and anywhere else online. On Twitter it's especially important that these links are shortened, because tweets are limited to 140 characters, and regular URLs can be lengthy.

Advanced Social Media Management and Tracking Software

While basic social media management software is good for scheduling posts and tracking clicks on links, a sport marketer can do a lot more with advanced software. Companies such as Argyle Social and Sprout Social sell software that can be used to set up campaigns, coordinate updates from multiple employees, utilize short links that integrate with website analytics software, and track conversions that are influenced by clicks on these links. If one goal of your social media program is to drive leads or conversions, and you'd like to be able to measure social media's impact on these, then it may make sense to step up to more advanced social media management and tracking software.

Companies that provide this type of advanced software usually have a link shortening/tracking solution that places a cookie on an individual's computer when he or she clicks a link. This enables an organization to understand not only which links get the most clicks, but also which types of content are driving the most sales, email signups, or donations. With the proper setup, the organization should be able to see the sales that were influenced by these links, even if people clicked the link but did not purchase something immediately.

Advanced social media management tools also give sport organizations the ability to group social content and links into campaigns. This enables the organization to see which campaigns are driving the most clicks, interactions, and sales over time.

Here's how this could work for a sport-related nonprofit organization that is trying to increase donations. The organization may be posting a variety of content to Facebook and Twitter. Some of it may be funny, some may be informative, and some may be newsworthy. It may consist of links to blog posts, pictures, and videos. By grouping similar content together in campaigns, the organization will be able to tell which types (e.g., informative videos or funny pictures) are generating the most clicks, interactions, and donations over a given time period.

Social media measurement checklist

- Define your program's objective.
- Pick an approach (direct ROI, correlated ROI, or both).
- Agree on key metrics and how often to measure them.
- Choose the right tools.
- Establish a baseline.
- Measure and share findings.

Surveys

Surveys offer a chance to obtain insights on fan behavior, attitudes, and preferences, which is especially helpful if the goal of your social media program is to change any of these attributes. For example, a youth sport league may wish to learn which social media tools parents use most so it can engage with other parents to build awareness about the league using those tools.

When conducting a survey, let people know what the survey's purpose is, avoid using jargon or confusing language, and keep the survey as short as possible. Most people do not want to spend 30 minutes on an online survey, and you may even need to provide an incentive, such as a gift certificate or entry into a sweepstakes, to get enough people to participate (Write Market, n.d.).

Other Tools

Here is a small sample of other online tools that may be useful as part of your social media measurement arsenal.

- **Klout.** This tool measures the online influence of a company or individual based on a variety of factors related to Twitter and Facebook audience size and engagement. This may be useful, for example, if an organization wants to get the word out about a new product and encourage coverage from industry bloggers. It may wish to look at a select group of bloggers and use their Klout scores (the higher the score, the better), as one way to determine who to prioritize for outreach.

- **Social Mention.** This tool calculates the number of times people mention your brand online, what topics they're talking about in relation to your brand, and the sentiment of these mentions. A word of warning—no automated sentiment tracking tool is 100 percent accurate. However, this tool is useful for seeing whether or not your social media efforts are leading to increased conversation about your brand or product.

- **Radian6, Sysomos, and other social media monitoring tools.** These tools can be helpful in measuring mentions of a company on a variety of social media channels, especially when there is a high volume of mentions each day or week. These tools are also helpful in discovering how a company's social media program, new marketing campaign, or product launch is affecting the level of conversation (and the sentiment of these conversations) about its brand and/or products.

These are just a few of the tools available for tracking social media metrics and KPIs. There are thousands of these tools, and the list is growing each day. Keep in mind that you should decide what you want to measure first, then choose the tools that will help you accomplish this. You don't need every tool or measurement software available; you just need the ones that help you measure whether you are meeting your objectives.

SOCIAL MEDIA MEASUREMENT CHALLENGES

Social media measurement is certainly growing in importance for sport marketers, especially as more teams, organizations, and agencies invest money into social media programs. However, accurately measuring the effectiveness of their social media programs presents some challenges.

Lack of Objectives in Social Media Programs

It's almost impossible to measure the effectiveness of a social media program if it has no agreed upon objectives. Nonetheless, many organizations enact social media strategies without written objectives, devoting time and resources to them without having a way to measure their effectiveness.

Choosing What to Measure Is Not Easy

It is not always apparent what should be measured, what measurement model to use, and which KPIs to track. To make things more complicated, social media is used not only as a marketing channel, but also for other purposes such as customer service and product development. Choosing metrics that match up with objectives and targets can certainly be challenging.

Correlation Can Be Difficult to Establish

Let's say a team notices that its ticket sales are up over the past six months. Fan engagement on Facebook, Twitter, and YouTube is also up over this period. It may be tempting to think that ticket sales are up as a result of the team's social media program, but this would be the wrong conclusion to draw without conducting further research. Ticket sales may have increased because of another marketing program. Or sales may be up because the team is winning. You cannot draw definite conclusions about the effectiveness of a social media program by examining correlated activities and results.

CONCLUSION

Properly planning a social media campaign, establishing objectives and targets for the program, and taking steps to measure its success are all vital to making sure social media efforts aren't going to waste. Measuring the effectiveness of social media programs may require a new way of thinking for some organizations, in addition to new tools. The bottom line is that social media measurement is a vital component of success. Don't let people tell you that social media can't be measured, and don't fall into the trap of looking only at social media metrics while ignoring actual business metrics.

As social media strategist Olivier Blanchard said, "only by establishing a relationship between social media metrics and business metrics will you be able to gauge both the impact and value (including but not limited to R.O.I.) of social media on your campaigns, programs and overall business" (2011b).

REVIEW QUESTIONS

1. What are the key considerations in planning an effective social media program?

2. Why is it important for a social media program to have objectives and targets?

3. What are two of the common approaches to social media measurement?

4. What are the challenges for sport organizations looking to measure the effectiveness of their social media programs?

REFERENCES

Bent Curve Media (n.d.). Case study: Dell outlet. Retrieved from http://www.bentcurve.com/smo/case-study-dell-outlet/.

Bernoff, J. (2007, December 7). The POST method: A systematic approach to social strategy. Retrieved from http://forrester.typepad.com/groundswell/2007/12/the-post-method.html.

Blanchard, O. (2011a). *Social media ROI: Managing and measuring social media efforts in your organization.* Boston, MA: Pearson.

Blanchard, O. (2011b, May 31). The basics of social media measurement for business. Retrieved from http://thebrandbuilder.wordpress.com/2011/05/31/the-basics-of-social-media-measurement-for-business/.

Briody, K. (2011, April 22). Social media ROI revisited: 4 ways to measure. Retrieved from http://www.ignitesocialmedia.com/social-media-measurement/social-media-roi-revisited-4-ways-to-measure/.

Manjoo, F. (2011, June 22). Does social media have a return on investment? Retrieved from http://www.fastcompany.com/magazine/157/joe-fernandez-klout-social-media.

National Sports Forum (2011, April 20). LA fans go "GAGA" over online contest. Retrieved from http://www.sports-forum.com/newsletter/previous/index.html?article_id=398.

Ostrow, A. (2009, December 8). Dell rides Twitter to $6.5 million in sales. Retrieved from http://mashable.com/2009/12/08/dell-twitter-sales/.

Schroeder, S. (2008, December 16). Twitter may have made Dell a million, it doesn't mean it can be (easily) monetized. Retrieved from http://mashable.com/2008/12/16/twitter-dell-million/.

Srabian, B. (2011, June 21). Personal interview by J Peck.

Werner, B. (2011, June 27). 2011 Catalyst fan engagement study. Retrieved from http://www.catalystpublicrelations.com/new-2011-catalyst-fan-engagement-study.

Write Market (n.d.). More tips on web survey design. Retrieved from http://www.thewritemarket.com/marketing/index.php?marketing=survey-tips&title=More%20Tips%20on%20Web%20Survey%20Design.

index